Living Vedanta

Amma & Advaita

By Swami Ramakrishnananda Puri

Mata Amritanandamayi Center, San Ramon
California, United States

Living Vedānta

Amma & Advaita

By Swami Ramakrishnananda Puri

Published By:
Mata Amritanandamayi Center
P.O. Box 613
San Ramon, CA 94583-0613, USA

In India:
www.amritapuri.org
inform@amritapuri.org

In Europe:
www.amma-europe.org

In US:
www.amma.org

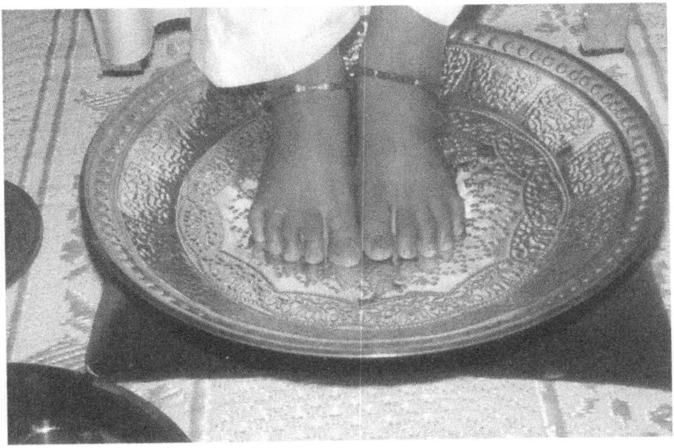

Offered at the Lotus Feet
of My Beloved Sadguru,
Sri Mata Amritanandamayi Devi

Contents

Sri Mata Amritanandamayi Devi

Through her extraordinary acts of love and self-sacrifice, Sri Mata Amritanandamayi Devi, or "Amma," as she is more commonly known, has endeared herself to millions around the world. Tenderly caressing everyone who comes to her, holding them close to her heart in a loving embrace, Amma shares her boundless love with all—regardless of their beliefs, their social status or why they have come to her. In this simple yet powerful way, Amma is transforming the lives of countless people, helping their hearts to blossom, one embrace at a time. In the past 45 years, Amma has physically hugged more than 40 million people from all parts of the world. Her tireless spirit of dedication to uplifting others has inspired a vast network of charitable activities, through which people discover the deep sense of peace and inner fulfillment that comes from selflessly serving others. Amma teaches that the divine exists in everything, sentient and insentient. Realizing this truth is the essence of spirituality—the means to end all suffering. Amma's teachings are universal. Whenever she is asked about her religion, she replies that her religion is love. She does not ask anyone to believe in God or to change their faith, but only to inquire into their own real nature and to believe in themselves.

Introduction

Whether we know it or not, we have only one goal in life: to be happy. We may pursue other goals, but if we analyze we will see that, ultimately, those goals are also attempts to find happiness. Subconsciously, our mind is constantly calculating whether or not our various actions will add to our happiness or detract from it.

Just pick six actions you did within the past 24 hours. Let's say: 1) showered and brushed your teeth; 2) did 20 minutes of meditation, 3) ate breakfast, 4) hugged a loved one, 5) went to work, and 6) spent an hour volunteering with a charitable organization. While the direct, intended benefit of each of these actions varies, the primary, indirect, intended benefit of all of them is happiness. You can say you brush your teeth because you want clean teeth and sweet-smelling breath, but why do we want those things? Very simple: Cavities are painful and detract from our happiness. Likewise, foul-smelling breath is embarrassing and, knowing we have it makes us self-conscious and detracts from our peace of mind.

Similarly, adhering to a meditation practice may or may not bring happiness in that moment, but people who meditate believe that, ultimately, it makes them happier and more peaceful—even if the practice itself at times feels tedious. Breakfast makes all of us happy. But let's say we skip breakfast. Then somewhere we have calculated that losing weight will bring us more happiness than pancakes. As a supermodel once controversially said, "Nothing tastes as good as skinny feels."

We may go to work for money and to contribute to society, but why do we want those things? We know that without money we will suffer. Moreover, many people feel unfulfilled if they are not actively contributing to society. We embrace our loved ones because maintaining those relationships by giving and receiving affection makes us feel whole and blissful. We even volunteer because we believe it will bring us happiness—the positive feelings that helping others generates inside of us.

I mentioned this point to a devotee once, and he said he didn't agree. He knew many people who volunteer only out of social pressure. But I pointed out that even that motivation is generated from the desire to attain happiness. We want to avoid the criticism of our peers. Our mind has calculated that failing to align with our peers' values will subtract from our happiness more than driving to the soup kitchen and, perhaps, missing the cricket match or basketball game. Ultimately, everything we do, we do for happiness.

Amma has her own unique way of expressing this. She says, "Our lives are meant to be born in love, to live in love and to eventually end in love." What is love? Love is happiness. They are synonyms. The feeling of love and the feeling of happiness are one and the same: bliss, peace, joy. As we say in Sanskrit, *ānanda*. But Amma's quote doesn't end there. She says, "Our lives are meant to be born in love, to live in love and to eventually end in love. But, tragically, even though most of us spend our lives in search of love, the majority of us die without ever finding it." Amma is saying that, even though all of our lives are aimed at experiencing love and happiness, we are failing miserably. Therefore, if our subconscious mind is constantly calculating what will bring us the most happiness, obviously there is a fundamental flaw in its mathematics.

This flaw is pointed out in the Madhu Brāhmaṇa of Bṛhadāraṇyaka Upaniṣad. In fact, here, we literally get to watch the evolution of a spiritual seeker's happiness formula. Having gained *ātma-jñānaṁ* [self-knowledge], Yājñavalkya has decided to divide his household possessions between his two wives in order to take up the life of a wandering monk. Yājñavalkya already understands his true nature, but he wants to fully dedicate his life to imbibing that understanding—to having it saturate his thoughts, words and deeds. He wants to reap the mental peace, contentment and happiness that come when self-knowledge expands to pervade the subconscious.

When he informs his two wives of this, one—Kātyāyanī—is content with his decision. The other, Maitreyī, realizes that if her husband is willing to walk away from all of his possessions and relationships, he must possess something much more valuable. So, she inquires, "Forget half of your stuff... If I had all the possessions in the world, would it free me from death?" Yājñavalkya readily admits that it would not.

"It would make you very comfortable," he says. "But one day you will still die." Hearing this, Maitreyī understands that no matter how much comfort and happiness she can get from relationships and possessions, they will all disappear when she is separated from them in death. Her mind is running a happiness calculation: "How much happiness can I get for how long from all Yājñavalkya's stuff?" She realizes, "Not that much and not for very long."

Pleased with his wife's spiritual maturity, Yājñavalkya begins to instruct her about the nature of happiness and its connection with material possessions and relationships:

> sa hovaca na vā are patyuḥ kāmāya patiḥ priyo bhavatyātmanastu kāmāya patiḥ priyo bhavati | na vā are jāyāyai kāmāya jāyā priyā bhavatyātmanastu kāmāya jāyā priyā bhavati |

> Yājñavalkya said, 'It is not, my dear, out of love for the husband that he is cherished but out of love for one's self. Nor, my dear, is it out of love for the wife that she is cherished but out of love for one's self that she is dear.[1]

1 Bṛhadāraṇyaka Upaniṣad, 4.5.6

This is a hard truth to accept, but for a spiritual seeker, an important one. Everyone has only one true love: It is, was and always will be we ourselves alone. All other forms of love are secondary or subsidiary to the foundation of self-love.

In fact, Advaita Vedānta tells us that a human being is capable of loving only two things: the experience of happiness itself and the various means to attain the experience of happiness. Thus, in the *mantra*, Yājñavalkya is giving Maitreyī insight into the nature of relationships, including that of their own soon-to-be-ending marriage. He is telling her, "Look, you may think you love me, but really you only love the happiness that my presence and actions, etc, generate in your mind. You love me as an efficient means to that happiness experience. That's also why I've 'loved' you and Kātyāyanī as well."

Yājñavalkya's teaching may seem quite harsh. It almost sounds nihilistic, but hidden within it is a true diamond of wisdom, light and love. For, Yājñavalkya is not just saying that love is "selfish" with a small "s"; he is also saying love is "Selfish" with a capital "S."

Means, love is of the nature of the Self—the True Self, the *ātmā*. That love you think you get through possessions and relationships, in fact, is not coming from those objects at all; it is coming from within. It is the manifestation in our mind of the bliss that is our true nature. It is *that* experience—the experience of one's mind reflecting the bliss of the *ātmā*—that we love and crave. We mistake its source to be outside. In reality, that bliss is who we are.

This mistake is why our happiness formulas keep failing—because our formula places the highest value on the various means to happiness and not on happiness itself. And all the means in our calculations—money, houses, health, relationships, entertainment, pleasure, etc—are limited. Therefore, they can only create the conditions for a limited amount of happiness to manifest in our mind for a limited amount of time. If we want to attain ultimate happiness—true bliss—then we have to understand and assimilate happiness not as coming through external means, but as our fundamental nature. As Amma says, "We need to shift from 'I love you' to 'I am love.'"

This shift cannot be achieved through any action—secular or sacred—because it is not a physical shift. It is a shift in knowledge; we have to understand that love is already our true nature. So, it is, as said in Vedānta, *prāptasya prāptiḥ*—attainment of the already attained. It is discovering the truth: "I am, was and always will be the one infinite, eternal wellspring of love and bliss."

For example, let's say there was a man named Cletus who somehow didn't know he was a human being. He thought he was a Labrador Retriever. One day, however, he gets it into his head that he would like to become a human being. Cletus decides that this is actually his true purpose in life. Nothing else matters. He wants to do everything he can to make it happen as soon as possible.

Now, how is Cletus going to accomplish this? If he walks 10,000 miles will he become human? No, he will not. What if he stops eating dog food and becomes vegetarian? No. What if he learns to meditate and does so for 20 hours straight while performing "downward-facing human" *yogāsana*? No. None of these things can make Cletus human. Why? Because Cletus already is human. He is a human being who *thinks* he is a dog. So, nothing can "make" Cletus a human being, not even the knowledge he is a human being. Because he already is a human being.

This is the foundational premise of Advaita Vedānta. Not that we are humans thinking we are dogs, but that we are all God—the one, all-pervasive divinity—thinking we are human. As Amma says, "Divinity is your true nature. Nothing can change that. If you insist on saying, 'I am the ego, body, mind and intellect,' it won't make any difference. Your true nature isn't the least affected by your lack of understanding. It is like saying that the earth is flat and not round. If you keep preaching that the earth is flat, believing it to be true, is it going to change the shape of the earth in any way? No, of course not. Similarly, you are free to believe that you are the ego and that the ego is real, but you will, nevertheless, continue to remain what you are: the *ātmā*. Your divine nature will not change or be diminished, even if you don't believe in it."

Thus, just as we can believe we are a dog or a human and the reality remains the same, it also remains the same whether we believe we are the ego or the *ātmā*. The truth is not affected by either our ignorance or by our knowledge.

Why then does Vedānta stress knowledge so much? Because when we understand our true nature, life becomes full and complete. We realize that the love and happiness we were searching for our entire life is not outside of us. That love is we ourselves—God. It is in this knowledge that we become fulfilled. The constant struggle for contentment ends. Thereafter, our actions cease to be aimed at taking and become aimed at giving. We no longer act out of a sense of lack but out of a sense of fullness anod completion. We become someone like Amma, whom the scriptures describe as embodiments of altruism:

śāntā mahānto nivasanti santaḥ
vasantavalloka-hitaṁ carantaḥ |
tīrṇāḥ svayaṁ bhīmabhavārṇavaṁ janān
ahetunānyānapi tārayantaḥ ||

There are peaceful, magnanimous people, who live, like the spring season, doing good to

> others, and who, having crossed this dreadful ocean of worldly existence themselves, help others also to cross the same, without any selfish motive whatsoever.[2]

Thus, just as only the knowledge, "Cletus, you are not a dog; you are a human being," can figuratively liberate Cletus from being a dog, so too *ātma-jñānam* alone figuratively liberates us from the misconception that we are human beings—limited, mortal, bound and suffering. This shift in our self-understanding itself is what we refer to as *mokṣa*—liberation. This is why the *gurus* of the Advaita Vedānta lineage firmly state: *kevalād-eva jnānād-mokṣaḥ*—"From knowledge alone comes liberation."[3]

The title of this book is *Living Vedānta*. It was chosen because this is what we see in Amma—someone whose every thought, action and word is completely in tune with the principles of Vedānta. Moreover, whenever Amma discusses Advaita, she stresses that

---

2 Vivekacūḍāmaṇi, 37

3 Ādi Śaṅkarācārya's introductory commentary to the third chapter of the Bhagavad-Gītā.

ultimately Vedānta is not something to just talk about, but is something to be lived. Amma says, "The ancient sages did eons of intense spiritual practices. They actually *lived* Vedānta. Most of us merely read and lecture about the scriptures. This is an intellectual exercise. Vedānta has to be lived. This is true spirituality. The only way we can truly judge our spiritual progress is by assessing our ability to be equanimous and patient regardless of the circumstances and by the love and compassion for others that spontaneously wells up in our heart. These need to be our primary focus."

Hence, the aim of this book is to present the essence of spiritual knowledge, a brief overview of the process of obtaining it and to reveal how Advaita is Amma's ultimate teaching. Moreover, we will also investigate what Amma means when she speaks of "living Vedānta" and why she feels it is of such critical importance for the spiritual seeker.

1

The Goddess of Knowledge

In Indian culture, knowledge is considered supreme—higher than anything. It is even deified and worshipped as Goddess Sarasvatī, the Divine Mother. Whenever we have any gathering or program, we begin with the lighting of the oil lamp. Its flame represents knowledge. The resolve behind lighting it is: "As this flame illumines this dark room, may this knowledge spread to us all and remove the darkness of ignorance." The ancient poet Bhatṛhari once praised knowledge with the following couplet:

na cora-hāryaṁ na ca rāja-hāryaṁ
na bhrātṛ-bhājyaṁ na ca bhārakārī |
vyaye kṛte vardhata eva nityaṁ
vidyā-dhanaṁ sarva-dhana-pradhānam ||

Not subject to theft, nor to taxation; not claimable by a brother, nor ever a burden. It always grows when used. The wealth of knowledge is the greatest of all forms of wealth.

Ultimately, knowledge is allotted such a high status in Indian culture because of its tremendous transformative power. It is our understanding of objects, people and God, etc, that creates our attitudes towards them. In turn, it is our attitudes that instigate our thoughts, words and actions. Thus, knowledge is the foundation of our entire life. Through its expansion, comes total transformation. Currently our knowledge about ourselves and the world is faulty. As such, our interactions with the world and each other are problematic. Only when we correct our misunderstandings regarding our own nature and the nature of the world, will our actions become harmonious, like Amma's.

The following example, which Amma herself has used, illustrates this truth: Amma says, "Once, a school was faced with a unique problem. A number of girls were beginning to use lipstick and were putting it on in the bathroom. That was fine, but after they put on their lipstick, they would press their lips to the mirror to remove the excess. This was leaving dozens of little lip prints on the mirror. At the end of each day, the janitor had to spend hours cleaning the lip prints off the mirrors. He tried to tell the students. He put signs up in the bathrooms and on the noticeboards. But no one cared. Finally, he made an official complaint to the principal. Soon, she came to inspect the students' handiwork. She consoled the janitor and told him that she would call all the students and take care of it.

"The next day, the principal called all the girls into the bathroom and met them there with the janitor. She first explained that all these lip prints were causing a major problem for him, as he had to clean all the mirrors every day. But none of the students were really paying attention.

"Amused by their lack of interest, the principal called the janitor and asked him to demonstrate how he cleaned the mirrors. He then took out a long-handled squeegee, dipped it down into a toilet, lifted it up and then used it to clean the mirror.

"The girls screamed, 'Yuck! Is this way that the mirrors are cleaned?'

"The janitor said, 'Yes, the mirrors are cleaned this way every day.'

"Needless to say, there were never any lip prints on the mirror again."

When telling this story, Amma says, "The principal's *satsaṅg* and the girls' realization went together hand in hand. They understood in a flash, and it instantly and immediately transformed their thinking, their feelings and their actions."

This is the power of knowledge. The girls all had a certain concept of the bathroom mirror—that it was pure. Seeing their own freshly made-up faces shining in it, they felt an attitude of love for their reflection. Consequently, this attitude inspired them to kiss their reflection. Thus, knowledge dictated attitude; attitude dictated action. But then the principal and janitor revealed to the girls that their understanding regarding the mirror was flawed. The mirror was not pure; it was smeared with toilet water. With their new understanding of the mirror's nature, the girls' attitude towards the mirror changed from attraction to disgust. And immediately their actions changed.

Like light, knowledge illumines and clarifies previously misunderstood things. Yet among all fields of knowledge, self-knowledge is special; it totally transforms us. It does so because it completely changes, once and for all, our concept of who we are. There is no end to other forms of learning. In fact, when it comes to studying material sciences, the more we learn the more we realize we do not know. If we come to material science with a sense of inner incompleteness, our study will not change that. We may become knowledgeable about history, physics, nanoscience or chemistry, etc, but we will continue to feel alienated, lonely, depressed, incomplete.

This is described beautifully in Chāndogya Upaniṣad. There, Nārada, a very learned man, approaches a sage named Sanatkumāra. Nārada has heard of his greatness and wants to become his disciple. He introduces himself and soon is enumerating all of his various accomplishments and achievements in life. It is quite a long list: all the subjects he has studied, all the arts he has mastered, the various sciences and branches of knowledge, the degrees he's attained, etc. It's quite an impressive list. It seems to go on forever. But then, after enumerating this massive list, Nārada confesses: *so 'haṁ bhagavaḥ śocāmi*—"Venerable one, I'm still sad." The Upaniṣad then explains that knowledge is indeed the answer, but not material knowledge. What is needed is not knowledge of objects, but knowledge of the subject itself: *tarati śokam ātmavit*—"The knower of the self crosses over sorrow."[1] This is the essence of spirituality. Amma says the exact same thing: "When we lead our life with the knowledge that *ātmā* is the real source of eternal peace, then we can avoid or overcome sorrow." In fact, I remember once a journalist asked Amma to explain the essence of spirituality in just one phrase. Amma's answer was: "Know your self."

Like Nārada, we have accomplished many things in life. The problem is that we expected lasting happiness from those accomplishments. Studying art and literature and learning about the world and science is wonderful. These can enrich our life in many ways, but they are not going to bring us true, lasting happiness. This is not because of any failing of ours, but because they are incapable of doing so. Expecting geniune

[1] Chāndogya Upaniṣad, 7.1.3

happiness from such accomplishments is like expecting jewelry at the post office.

It seems once two economists were walking in a park when one said to the other, "If you let me punch you in the face, I'll give you $5,000." The second economist thinks for a minute, then agrees. *Boom!* He's punched in the face. The first economist writes him a check for $5,000, and they keep going. A few minutes later, the second economist says, "Hey, if you let me punch you in the face, I'll give you $5,000." The first economist agrees, and—*Boom!*—he is punched in the face. Walking a little further, the first economist stops. He looks at his friend. They both have bloody noses. He says, "I can't help but feel like we both just got punched in the face for no reason at all." The second economist responds, "What? We single-handedly increased the GDP by $10,000!"

The point is, material pursuits and objective knowledge have their own value. But from the standpoint of happiness, that value is theoretical at best.

Vedānta tells us that we are moving through life with a fundamental misunderstanding about the world and its objects as well as about our own nature—who we are. Unfortunately, these misunderstandings are dictating our attitudes towards the world and towards ourselves. Moreover, those attitudes, which are based on confusion, are charting the very course of our life. If we can correct those misunderstandings, our negative attitudes will become positive, and our life will find peace and harmony. Our sorrow will disappear. For this to happen, knowledge alone is required—true knowledge about ourselves.

Let me conclude this chapter with an example: Once a man went for his yearly physical. The doctor ran some tests and told him to return the following week. A week later, the man returns and is called into the doctor's office. The doctor tells him to sit down across from him and begins to look intensely at his computer screen. Suddenly the doctor frowns. He says, "No, no, no, this is no good at all."

The man is instantly petrified. "What is it, doctor? Is it cancer?"

"What?" says the doctor. "No, you're fine. My golfing buddy just changed our tee time."

Vedānta says we are all like this patient. Misunderstanding the nature of the world and who we are, we become filled with tension and anxiety. The doctor tells his patient, "No, You are fine," and instantly he finds peace. Similarly, once we properly understand and imbibe the message Amma and the scriptures are telling us, we will also find peace. "Don't worry; you are fine" is the essential teaching of Vedānta. The difference between the doctor's diagnosis and Vedānta's is that the doctor is speaking about the body. Vedānta is speaking about our True Self—the *ātmā*. The body will be healthy at times and unhealthy at others, but the *ātmā* is eternal, ever devoid of affliction, ever pure, ever blissful and ever free.

2

The Scissors of Viveka

Self-knowledge is very subtle. This is because the object of the knowledge is not an object at all; it is the subject. Think of all the various forms of knowledge we currently may possess: knowledge of sports, of music, of geography, of our relatives, of material science, of math, etc. In all of these examples, the object of our knowledge is something different from us. We know this because when we take up each field of study, we have two different things: I, the subject, and then the science, the object of my study. Molecular biology, the study of the inner workings of molecules, is a subtle science when compared to, say, gross anatomy. And psychology could be considered even subtler since it deals with something not even microscopic but invisible—the inner workings of our mind. But subtler than all of these is the study of the *ātmā*. As subtle as the mechanics of a molecule may be, they are still objectifiable. Likewise, we may not be able to see the psyche, but we can see its effects. The *ātmā,* however, is imperceptible regardless of how state-of-the-art our scientific instruments may be. Because it has no qualities to perceive. Thus, the Upaniṣads declare that the *ātmā* is *anubhyo 'aṇu*—"Subtler than the subtle."[1] And: *naiva vācā na manasā prāptuṁ śakyo na cakṣuṣā*—"It cannot be attained by speech, the mind or by the eye."[2] And: *yato vāco nivartante, aprāpya manasā saha*—"Failing to reach the *ātmā*, words turn back along with the mind."[3]

Amma says the same thing. She says, "Science deals with the objective world, whereas spirituality deals with the subjective world—the essence of one's existence. The former is all about the seen—the world. The latter is entirely about the seer—the indwelling self, without which the diverse world of names and forms does not exist. One is gross, and the other, subtle. So, knowing the *ātmā* is not as easy as knowing the body and the desires associated with it. People naturally pursue the known rather than the unknown,

---

1 Muṇḍaka Upaniṣad, 2.2.2
2 Kaṭha Upaniṣad, 2.3.12
3 Taittirīya Upaniṣad, 2.9.1

which, in reality, is one's own True Self. Thus, they gravitate towards the gross objects of the world rather than towards the subtle principles of spirituality and life."

Hearing such statements may irritate us. After all, we are told we cannot touch the *ātmā*. Nor can we see it or hear it, etc. Moreover, it cannot even be an object of thought. At the same time, we are told that knowing it is the only way to attain the peace, happiness and sense of completion that our entire life has been dedicated to attaining. It sounds like a paradox. We may feel like the young woman who, upon being hired, is told by her new boss, "Forget everything you learned in college. It's all useless here!" The woman says, "But I never went to college." To which the boss replies, "You're fired. We only hire graduates."

Don't worry. Feeling our frustration, the scriptures tell us where to start. They say, if you cannot know the *ātmā* directly as "It is *this*." Then why not try to know it in reverse—by knowing everything it is not: "It is *not* this." If we can cross things off in this manner, maybe eventually we can arrive at our true nature by the process of elimination. Of course, no one identifies with the external world; the problem is our identification with the various aspects of our body-mind complex.

In the scriptures this method is presented through different models. Some of these include: *pañca-kośa viveka*—discrimination between the self and the five sheaths; *śarīra-traya viveka*—discrimination between the self and the gross, subtle and causal bodies; and *avasthā-traya viveka*—discriminating between the self and the waking state, dream state and deep-sleep state. These are all different methods to attain the same goal. Through each system, we become clear that our body-mind complex is not the self. That is why, in general, we refer to these systems as *ātma-anātma viveka*—discrimination between the self and non-self.

In his comprehensive Advaitic treatise Vivekacūḍāmaṇi, Śrī Ādi Śaṅkarācārya spends more than 50 verses presenting a very thorough version of the *pañca-kośa viveka.*[4] It is a very

4 The original source of the *pañca-kośa viveka* is found in the second chapter of Taittirīya Upaniṣad, known as the Brahmānanda Vallī.

helpful system which divides the human personality into five *kośas* [sheaths], each one subtler than the previous. These are the *annamaya kośa*—the food sheath, i.e. the physical body that has as its basis the food we eat; the *prāṇamaya kośa*—the energy sheath, which controls all of our neurological, cardiovascular, endocrinological systems, etc; the *manomaya kośa*—the mental sheath, comprising the sense organs along with all of our thoughts and emotions; the *vijñānamaya kośa*—the sheath that comprises our sense of self as a distinct individual, the ego who wills action and believes, "I am the thinker, the agent of action and the experiencer"; and finally the *ānandamaya kośa*—the sheath of experiential bliss.

In the text, Śaṅkarācārya elaborately explains each *kośa* as well as why none of them can be the *ātmā*. For example, he presents 10 reasons why the *ātmā* cannot be the *annamaya kośa*—the physical body:[5] 1) The *ātmā* is eternal, and the body clearly is not, 2)The *ātmā* is pure, and the physical body is full of impurities, 3) The *ātmā* is sentient, and the physical body

[5] Vivekacūḍāmaṇi, 154-164

is inert, 4) There are many different physical bodies and yet only one *ātmā*, 5) The physical body has attributes, and the *ātmā* is devoid of attributes, 6) The *ātmā* is changeless, and the physical body is constantly changing, 7)The physical body has no independent reality and the *ātmā* is the sole independent reality, 8) The physical body has parts, such as arms and legs, and the *ātmā* is partless, 9) The physical body is controlled, whereas the *ātmā*, is the controller, and 10) The *ātmā* is imperceptible, and we can all clearly see our bodies.

Śaṅkarācārya's arguments are logical. However, the logic is often a special type of logic—one founded on knowledge and faith in the statements of the scriptures. For example, take his argument that the physical body must be different from the *ātmā* because the *ātmā* is eternal and the physical body is not eternal. The mortality of the physical body is clear. We are all abundantly aware of the fact this flesh and bone will eventually die and, if not burned, will rot. We can logically arrive at this conclusion through analysis of all the physical bodies we see in the world. They all die. Therefore, we can logically infer that ours will also die. However, that the nature of the self is eternal—how do we know that? It is a matter of faith. Our only source for this information is the scriptures and the teachings of *mahātmās* like Amma. If we study them, we will see the Bhagavad-Gītā says:

> na jāyate mriyate vā kadācit
> nāyaṁ bhūtvā'bhavitā vā na bhūyaḥ |
> ajo nityaḥ śāśvato'yaṁ purāṇo
> na hanyate hanyamāne śarīre ||
>
> Never is this one born, and never does it die; nor is it that having come to exist, it will again cease to be. This one is birthless, eternal, nondecaying, ancient; it is not killed when the body is killed.[6]

And what did Amma say when, as a teenager, some villagers came to kill her because she would not stop giving *darśan*? She smiled and said, "I'm not afraid of death. You can kill this body, but the *ātmā* is immortal, indestructible. You cannot kill the *ātmā*." (What compassion Amma has! Kṛṣṇa may have taught Arjuna

---

[6] Bhagavad-Gītā, 2.20

ātma-jñānam on the battlefield, but Amma even tried to give self-knowledge to her would-be murderers.)

Thus, to deploy this logic—that the physical body cannot be the *ātmā* because it is not eternal like the *ātmā*—we have to have studied the scriptures and words of *mahātmās* like Amma. Not only should we have studied them, we need to have faith in them as well. Once that foundation is there, then we can compare and contrast the nature of the self—immortality—with the nature of the physical body—mortality—and conclude that this physical body cannot be the *ātmā*. In terms of pure logic, the best we could say would be, "If there truly is something called the *ātmā* that is immortal, then it would have to be different from this physical body, which is clearly mortal."

For example, I can tell you that the Upaniṣads say *prajñānaṁ brahma*—"Consciousness is brahman."[7] If you have faith in the scriptures, this is a powerful statement. But if you do not, you may turn around and say, "That is very nice, Swāmīji. In *Star Wars: Episode IV – A*

[7] Aitareya Upaniṣad, 3.1.3

New Hope, Obi Wan Kenobi says, 'The Force will be with you, always,' but I'm not going to base my life on that!" Therefore, since many people reading this book may be unversed in the Indian scriptures, and for the purpose of brevity, the system of *ātma-anātma viveka* we will use is called *dṛg-dṛśya viveka*—discrimination between the seer and the seen. This system is purely logical and does not require any scriptural knowledge to proceed.

Dṛg-dṛśya viveka is based on a few logical principles: 1) A substance and its attributes can never be physically separated. 2) Because a substance and its attributes cannot be physically separated, they must be experienced together. 3) If the substance and its attributes together comprise an experienced object, then there must be an experiencer-subject different from both the substance and its attributes. 4) Therefore, all experienced attributes belong to an experienced substance, and they can never belong to me, the experiencer-subject.

Let us see the first step: *A substance and its attributes can never be physically separated.* We can make this clear with an example—fire.

What are the main attributes of fire? Heat and light. We cannot have cold fire or dark fire. Now, can we separate those attributes from their substance? Can we cleave the property of "heat" away from fire and set it side by side with the object fire? No, that's impossible. Even though, perhaps, intellectually we can delineate the substance "fire" from the attribute "heat," we cannot physically separate them. The relationship between a substance and its attributes is therefore called a *samavāya saṁbandha*—an inherent relationship. Thus, this is our first logical law: *A substance and its attributes can never be physically separated.*

Our next step is an extension of that first law. Think of a series of attributes: fat, skinny, black, red, round, soft, sharp... None of these attributes can be experienced devoid of a substance. If I were to say to you, "Did you feel the pointy?" it makes no sense. You would immediately ask, "The pointy what?" This is because—as we just stated—an attribute can never be physically separated from its substance. And yet, we experience pointy things, red things, skinny things, round things. Thus, if we can experience the attribute of pointiness, and we know that no attribute can be separated from its substance, then we arrive at the extension: *All experienced attributes belong to experienced substances.* So, I cannot experience the pointiness of the needle, without simultaneously experiencing the needle itself. Likewise, I cannot experience the needle without experiencing its pointiness. The experience of the substance and its attribute is one experience alone. So, *all experienced attributes belong to experienced substances.*

Next comes a second logical law, which is very important to Advaita: *The experienced-object can never be the experiencer-subject.* An experiencer can never become its own object of experience. For example, take the eye—our organ of sight. In its own relative way, this organ is an experiencer-subject. With its power of sight, it can see, veritably, an infinite number of objects: the TV, the door, our family members, our own hands and feet, the clouds in the sky, the mountain in the distance, and even light being emitted from stars trillions of miles away. In the right circumstances, one eyeball can even see our other eyeball. But there is one thing an eyeball cannot see: an eyeball cannot directly see itself. So, *no experienced-object can ever be the experiencer-subject*.

Now, the final step: Since all experienced attributes—fatness, tallness, roundness, hotness, coldness, etc—belong to experienced substances, therefore, *no experienced attribute can belong to me, the experiencer-subject*.

If we take the *pañca-kośas* one by one, what do we see? Our skin may be black, brown or white. It may have moles, freckles or scars. It may be hairy, smooth, wrinkly... Regardless, all of these are attributes and are thus part and parcel of the substance called the body. That singular experience of the body and its attributes is clearly an object of my experience. Therefore—*since no experienced attribute can belong to me, the experiencer-subject*—the body and its attributes cannot be me. If we are trying to ascertain who we are by the process of elimination, then through this logical process we can definitely cross off the body.

Similarly, to some extent, we can experience the attributes of *prāṇamaya-kośa*—the energy flowing through the body. This energy reflects in our digestion, our heartrate, blood-pressure, temperature, the speed of our breathing. All these attributes belong to the substance of bodily energy. I can experience them. Therefore, those attributes and the substance cannot be me.

What about the mind—the *manomaya kośa*? It is also a substance with attributes that are experienced by us. Someone may ask us, "How are you?" And we say, "Oh, very happy," or maybe, "I'm a bit sad today." We experience the attributes of happiness and sorrow. Similarly, we experience when our memory is quick or slow, when we are filled with doubt or conviction. All of this is clearly observed by us. Conviction, doubt, desire, happiness, frustration, depression, sorrow, elation, jealousy, greed, etc—these are all attributes that belong to the substance called "mind." In clearly experiencing them, I am also experiencing the substance itself. Since no experienced object can be the experiencer-subject, this means that even the mind—with all its changing attributes—cannot be me.

The next level of our personality is the *vijñānamaya-kośa*. It includes the intellect and what is referred to as the *ahaṅkāra*—the ego. It is the *vijñānamaya-kośa* that gives us the sense of being a finite individual endowed with the qualities of *kartṛtvaṁ*, *bhoktṛtvam* and *pramātṛtvam*—agency, enjoyership and cognizance. It is this aspect of our personality that says, "*I* am doing this," "*I* experienced that," "*I* am thinking like this." If we are identified with the *manomaya kośa* when we become identified with emotions such as jealousy, then the *vijñānamaya kośa* is the thought "I am the one who is jealous."

Each sheath inward gets subtler and subtler. As such, each sheath successively becomes more difficult to cleave away from the True Self—the *ātmā*. But here too, we should acknowledge that the mere fact that we can talk about this aspect of our personality indicates that we experience it as an object of our awareness. Moreover, don't the convictions "I am doing this," "I am experiencing this," I am thinking this," come and go from our experience? Certainly, in deep sleep, the sense of self as a limited individual separate from everything else dissolves. Then upon waking, it immediately again manifests. Yet we miraculously retain a vague memory of a nontemporal experience wherein it was absent—wherein we knew nothing but a blank, fathomless bliss. Thus, even though the *ahaṅkāra* is very subtle, it is clearly an object of our awareness nonetheless. Śaṅkarācārya points this out in his concluding commentary on the Bhagavad-Gītā:

> When the continuous delusion that "the body, etc, is the *ātmā*" gets cut in deep sleep or in *samādhi*, etc, then the ills that are the sense of agency and enjoyership cease to be perceived.[8]

Amma also uses the experience in deep sleep to reveal to us that the ego and its concepts of "I" and "mine" are a transient experience, and, therefore, cannot be we—the subject. Amma says, "A child wants a doll so much that she cries for several hours. She finally gets a doll and plays with it for some time. She won't allow anyone else to touch it. She goes to sleep hugging the doll close to her. But then, as she sleeps, the doll slips to the floor and the child isn't even aware of it. Or a man hides his gold beneath his pillow

[8] Śaṅkarācārya's commentary following Bhagavad-Gītā, 18.66

and goes to sleep with his head resting on the pillow. But while he sleeps, a thief comes and steals it all. When he was awake, the man could think of nothing but his gold, and because of that he had no peace. But in his sleep, he forgot everything; he wasn't aware of himself or his family or his possessions. Once we wake up, '*my* doll,' '*my* necklace' and '*my* family' all come back. As the sense of 'I' returns, everything else returns along with it."

Finally, we arrive at the subtlest of all the *kośas*, the *ānandamaya-kośa*. Literally "the bliss sheath," the *ānandamaya-kośa* is perceived anytime we experience happiness, joy, bliss. It is experienced most profoundly in deep sleep, but anytime we become lost in joy through attaining something we desire, that is the experience of *ānandamaya-kośa*. We cannot actively, over an expanse of time, observe the deep-sleep state because during deep sleep, the mind with its capacity to evaluate time has temporarily resolved. However, upon waking, we miraculously have a vague memory of having experienced bliss. Why else do you think we enjoy sleeping so much? Why do we say, "No!

Just five more minutes!" when someone tells us we have to get up? It is because in dreamless sleep, we temporarily merge into a sea of bliss. Amma says, "In deep sleep, there is only bliss. The bliss we experience in deep sleep is what gives us the energy we feel when we wake up." In those periods of deep sleep, the mind resolves. Along with it, resolve our perception of time and space. Yet we do still experience the *ānandamaya kośa* nonetheless. We know this because all of us wake with that vague memory of "I knew nothing; I was in bliss." We remember it as an experience—just one stripped of time and space. The fact that we have that memory proves that the bliss experienced in deep sleep is different from us.

The question may arise: "How can I remember something that happened when the mental equipment responsible for recording memories was resolved when it took place?" While we cannot say exactly "how" that has occurred, we have to presume it occurred; otherwise, none of us would have that memory. In Indian epistemology, we refer to this means of knowing as *arthāpatti*—presumption. The classic example is that if an individual is fat and he never eats anything during the day, then we can presume that he eats at night. Likewise, if we all have a memory of having experienced bliss during deep sleep, even if we can't explain how that memory has occurred, we must somehow have experienced bliss.

And even in terms of the happiness we experience during the day—whether it is the happiness of receiving good news or eating ice cream or spending time with loved ones—that happiness is experienced as an object. How else could we grade it as we do? "Oh, I was happy then, but not like this!" etc. Even the bliss experienced by *yogīs* in *samādhi* is an object. That is why it comes when the *yogī* enters that state and leaves when he exits it. Regardless, be it in *samādhi*, deep sleep or upon learning we have won the lottery, any bliss we experience, by definition, has to be an object—an object of our experience. Therefore, it is an attribute of a substance—call it *ānandamaya kośa* or whatever else you like. I am experiencing the substance and its attributes. Therefore, it cannot be me—the subject.

Our problem is that we superimpose these external substances and their attributes—which are clearly objects of our experience—upon ourselves. But the mere fact that we experience them means they are clearly objects—not our self. In his commentary on Bṛhadāraṇyaka Upaniṣad, Śaṅkarācārya firmly rejects that anything experienced can be the self. There, he says even the statements "I don't know. I am confused," etc, do not reveal an attribute of the self, but reveal an experience of an attribute of the mind, which is distinct from the self—no different than the experience of a jar:

> "You say that a person feels, 'I do not know, I am confused': thereby you admit that he visualizes his ignorance and confusion; in other words, that these become the objects of his experience. So, how can ignorance and confusion, which are objects, be at the same time a description of the subject, the perceiver? If, on the other hand, they are a description of the subject, how can they be objects and be perceived by the subject? An object is perceived by an act of the subject. The

> object is one thing, and the subject another; it cannot be perceived by itself."[9]

Thus, through this logical process of *dṛg-dṛśya viveka*—discriminating the seer from the seen, the perceiver from the perceived, the knower from the known—we find that nothing we experience can be who we are. Vedānta asks: "How do you know it's not you?" And answers: "If you experience it, it's not you." All our physical attributes, belong to this physical body—not us. All our emotions and feelings, belong to the mind—not us. All our thoughts and ideas, belong to the intellect—not us. All experienced happiness is likewise an object—not us.

Learning to discriminate in this way is often referred to as the process of *neti neti*—"Not this, not this."[10] Amma herself often refers to this method of discriminating the not-self from the self. She even tells a story to illustrate it. "We need *viveka*," Amma says. "We need to understand that we are not this limited individual, but something beyond. We need to keep discriminating until

[9] Śaṅkarācārya's commentary on Bṛhadāraṇyaka, 4.4.6

[10] Bṛhadāraṇyaka Upaniṣad, 2.3.6

we have reached there. Once a son's father fell sick, and the son set out to get some medicine from the pharmacy. When he returned, the electricity had gone out. The room was pitch dark. After he reached the door, his challenge was to find his father because his father had to take the medicine immediately. The son entered his father's room, and he couldn't tell where his father's bed was. So, he kept reaching out and touching each and everything he could. He first reached the chair. 'This is not where my father is.' Then he reached the table. Again, 'This is the table. This is not where my father is.' Then he reached the cupboard and he said, 'This is the cupboard. This is not where my father is.' In this manner, he slowly made his way towards his father. Finally, he reached the bed and was able to give his father the medicine. In a similar way, we need to keep discriminating, *neti neti*—'I am not this, I am not this.' In this manner, we become clear, 'I am not the body, I am not the mind, I am not the intellect. My true nature is the *ātmā*.' If we keep discriminating in this way, we will gradually go beyond."

Through this process, we see that all the things we thought we were, we are not. Not the body, the mind, not the sense organs or the intellect. Not even the one who performs actions and reaps their results. Similarly, all the attributes of the mind: fear, jealousy, anger, depression, frustration, ignorance... Those are not my attributes. Those are all but changing attributes of the substance called "the mind." I am the witness of the mind and its changing attributes. In this manner, we arrive at a very enigmatic truth, which is diametrically opposite of how we originally thought. Previously we thought, "I experience sadness. Therefore, I am sad," And now, with the vision of Vedāntic discrimination, we realize, "I experience sadness; therefore, I am not sad." If the sorrowful one somehow was the *ātmā*, this would require another *ātmā* to know the sorrowful *ātmā*. If that *ātmā* wanted to be known, then yet another *ātmā* would be required, leading to the logical fallacy of infinite regress.

There is a story that illustrates this point: A businessman becomes deeply depressed. His entire life has been spent accumulating and accumulating, amassing more and more wealth. Then, one day, he falls sick. He goes to the doctor, and the doctor says, "I'm terribly sorry, but you have, maybe, six months to live—a year at best." The businessman's life flashes before his eyes. He realizes that all his money will soon be useless. His fancy cars, his Rolexes, his trophy wife—he won't be able to take any of it with him. For about one month, he wallows in depression. Then his friends, say, "Hey, you cannot keep living like this. I've heard of a *sādhu* who lives in a forest nearby. He is supposed to be very wise. Maybe he can help you."

So, they set off and soon enough find the *sādhu*. The man tells him his problem—both about his illness and about his deep depression. The *sādhu* says, "So, you are experiencing depression?" The businessman says, "Yes, that's why I came here. To get relief." The *sādhu* then says, "Well, if you experience depression, then you cannot be depressed." And the *sādhu* began explaining to the man all the things that we have been discussing: How the subject can never be its own object, etc. And the businessman suddenly becomes elated. He realizes that he was not depressed; his mind was depressed. And that understanding in itself somehow reduced the tumult his mind had been experiencing. Then he realized that even his illness belonged to the body—also not him. He—the True Self—was not sick at all. And this shift in understanding made him even happier. Finally, the businessman threw himself at the *sādhu*'s feet and said, "O Swāmīji, you are a true enlightened master. I am so blissful!" And to this the *sādhu* said, "No, you are not blissful. You are the one who is aware of the bliss that is reflecting in the mind. You, the eternal subject, can never be the object of your own experience."

3

A Cloth Cut in Half

Amma often tells us to employ *siṁhāvaloka-na-nyāya*—the maxim of the lion's backward glance. As a lion moves forward, occasionally, it will stop and look back over its shoulder. Amma says we should do the same thing in spiritual life. We must occasionally stop and look back to see where we have been and make sure we are still making progress. Thus, before moving forward here, let's review.

We want to know the true nature of the self because the *mahātmās* and scriptures have told us *tarati śokam ātmavit*—"The one who knows himself crosses over sorrow." But then we also have been told that we will never be able to know the self as an object of the mind or senses. As such, we have decided the best way to arrive at it is via the process of elimination—crossing off all the things that cannot be the self. For this purpose, we took up the method of distinguishing ourselves from all experienced objects. We did this by understanding the logical truth that the experiencer-subject can never be the experienced object. In this manner, we crossed off all the usual suspects: the physical body, the lifeforce maintaining the body, the mind and intellect, our sense of self endowed with the thoughts, "I am doing," "I am experiencing," and "I am thinking." We even negated experiential happiness as not-self. They all have the same sound alibi: "You experience me; therefore, I cannot be you."

It's here where some become disturbed. Because it is starting to sound like we are nothing at all—an onion without a center. Everything we have ever known has been logically negated and peeled away as "not me." The idea that, ultimately, we are nothing is called *śūnya-vāda*—the theory of the void. In fact, some great logicians have concluded this to be the reality. Luckily, even greater logicians, like Śaṅkarācārya, come to our rescue with the parable of the 10th man.

It seems 10 *brahmacārīs* wanted to go on a pilgrimage to a temple about a day's journey away. The *guru* put the eldest in charge and told him to ensure everyone returned in one piece. They set out by foot. After a few hours, the *brahmacārīs* came to a river and had no choice but to wade across. Climbing out onto the other bank, the leader figured it would be best to count everyone, just to make sure no one had drowned. But when he counted, he only located nine people. He began to panic. "Oh, no! One of us has drowned? Who is missing?" In a panic, he repeated his count, but again he only counted nine. Finally, a village boatman came by. Seeing the disciples in a panic, he asked what the problem was. The eldest *brahmacārī* told him. The boatman immediately broke out laughing, "Fool! You haven't counted yourself. You are the 10th man."[1]

This is exactly what happens to us when, after discerning ourselves from the *pañcakośas*, we panic and think, "My God! The nihilists were right; ultimately, there really is nothing but

[1] The parable of the 10th man is referenced by Śaṅkarācārya in his commentaries on Bṛhadāraṇyaka Upaniṣad, 1.4.7, and on Taittirīya Upaniṣad, 2.1.1, as well as in his treatise Upadeśa Sāhasrī. The full story is told in the seventh chapter of a 14th century treatise called the Pañcadaśī, written by Swāmī Vidyāraṇya.

nothingness!" Fortunately, just like the eldest disciple, here we are failing to count ourselves.

So, even in so-called *śūnyaṁ*—blankness, the void, emptiness—in reality, we are still there, observing the *śūnyam*. If we weren't, who is there to observe that *śūnyam*. Thus, even when everything we experience is crossed off, we ourselves—the ultimate subject, the observer, the witness-consciousness—remain. That is who we are: the pure, absolute consciousness that is never an object, but always the subject. As Amma says: "When you realize the truth that 'I am not the body; I am the self—the pure consciousness,' then true knowledge has dawned."

As simple as this seems on paper, this knowledge is not easy to assimilate. This is because, until now, everything we have ever known—since time immemorial—has been an object. Thus, it is only natural to want to know the *ātmā* as another object as well. However, "knowing the self" is not like knowing an object because the "thing" that we are to know is not a "thing" at all. It is the knower of all things. In all other forms of knowledge, we objectify the entity we are knowing; here, we grasp that it is the subject.

Negating all perceived phenomena and arriving at ourselves as being the witness consciousness is the essence of the *stotraṁ* written by Śaṅkarācārya that Amma regularly sings, Nirvāṇa Ṣaṭakam:

manobuddyahaṅkāra cittāni nāhaṁ
na ca śrotra-jihve na ca ghrāṇa-netre |
na ca vyoma bhūmirna tejo na vāyuḥ
cid-ānanda-rūpaḥ śivo'haṁ śivo'ham ||

na ca prāṇa-saṁjño na vai pañca-vāyuḥ
na vā sapta-dhātuḥ na vā pañcakośaḥ |
na vāk-pāṇi-pādaṁ na copasthapāyu
cid-ānanda-rūpaḥ śivo'haṁ śivo'ham ||

na me dveṣa-rāgau na me lobha-mohau
mado naiva me naiva mātsarya-bhāvaḥ |
na dharmo na cārtho na kāmo na mokṣaḥ
cidānanda-rūpaḥ śivo'haṁ śivo'ham ||

I am not the mind, intellect, *ahaṅkāra* or memory; not the ears or sense of taste, not the nose or eyes; I am not the elements of space, earth, fire or wind. I am Śiva whose nature is consciousness-bliss; I am Śiva.

> I am not what is called *prāṇa*, nor the five winds, nor the seven materials, nor the *pañcakośas*. I am not the organ of speech, the hands, feet, or sexual organ. I am Śiva whose nature is consciousness-bliss; I am Śiva.
>
> I have no likes or dislikes, no greed or delusion, no arrogance, nor even the feeling of jealousy. I have no need for *dharma*, security, pleasure or liberation. I am Śiva whose nature is consciousness-bliss; I am Śiva.

The process of negation described in these verses leaves us with the conviction that I am the only thing that remains when everything else is negated: I am the pure consciousness. But Śaṅkarācārya does not just say *cid-rūpa*—one's nature is consciousness. He says *cid-ānanda-rūpa*—whose nature is consciousness-bliss. And what did we start off searching for? Not consciousness. Our search—the search of all of humanity—is for bliss, happiness, peace, the feeling of an unfathomable love. Correct? Then where is bliss?

In truth, through this process of discrimination, *ātma-anātma viveka*, we can take a tremendous amount of peace and happiness. If we can conduct this process of discerning who we are from the body-mind complex, it is truly a big leap forward in our spiritual progress. Because from this alone, we come to understand that all of "our" so-called problems are not really "our" problems at all. Physical problems—health problems, beauty problems, etc—belong to either the physical or physiological body. Not me. Emotional problems—anger, jealousy, inferiority complex, anxiety—belong to the mind. Not me. So, too, cognitive problems, memory problems, problems in understanding, etc. Not me. And what about my relationship problems? Problems with friends and family and colleagues? Are these problems my problems—problems of pure consciousness? Impossible. All relationships are based on the body and mind—connections at a physical, emotional or intellectual level. So, such problems are also not my problems. As Amma says, "When we know that we are beyond this body—that we are that eternal principle, the supreme consciousness and nothing can touch our true nature—insecurity vanishes. With such a conviction, you can be fearless in each and every situation. Even if there was an earthquake or tsunami, you have the attitude of acceptance, understanding that everything can only harm the external realm, nothing can touch the real me. Then we will be able to overcome all kinds of fears and insecurities—be it fear of losing our position or fear of death. All such fears disappear when you know your true nature is beyond all these modifications. When you understand that this eternal principle cannot be touched by anything, you remain fearless in every situation. All experiences such as happiness and sorrow, insult and praise, heat and cold, birth and death, pass right through you. You remain beyond it all, as the witness—the very substratum of all experience, witnessing everything like a playful child."

Of course, it is in Amma that we see just how peaceful one can be when not identified with the body-mind complex and the world's never-ending problems. I will give on example. In Kerala, there is a lot of yellow press in the local language. The majority of these small tabloids are unabashedly ideology-driven. For whatever reason, the idea that there is such a thing as self-realization and that it culminates in divine altruism is an abomination to some of these groups. Thus, occasionally, they will target Amma with articles that have no basis in fact. Even recently someone wrote that Amma had proclaimed that she will never die because before she does she will turn herself into a black rock. (The guy who wrote this clearly has a rock for a brain.) Of course, Amma would never say anything like that. He just wanted to try to make Amma look bad in order to try to harm the faith of the devotees. Only then would the devotees perhaps consider siding with his political party, which is firmly atheistic and which says there is no such thing as self-realization.

About 30 years back, one such paper wrote a malicious story attacking Amma's character. We hardly had newspapers in the *āśraṁ* back then, but some devotees who had read the article were very hurt and informed me. Reading what they wrote, I also became angry. As soon as I got a chance, I went to Amma to explain what had been written. The main allegation was that Amma and the *āśraṁ* residents had dug a tunnel under the *āśraṁ* via which drugs were smuggled out to the middle of the Arabian Sea, where a ship, captained by the CIA, would come and whisk them away to America. The "journalist" had also disrespectfully used Amma's given name: Sudhamani.

When I finished informing Amma, she said, "But, son, you know none of those things are true. Why does it bother you?"

I said, "Amma, let that be. I cannot bear this insult to your name."

And then Amma said something that very much took me aback. "Why should it insult me? I am not Sudhamani?"

This was an expression of Amma's *viveka.* Amma was reminding me that she is identified with the pure consciousness that is the self. If someone thinks they are attacking Amma by mocking or slandering this five-foot-tall female body with dark skin and a nose ring, then he is a fool.

It's like the time a filmmaker making a documentary on interreligious harmony asked Amma to introduce herself by saying, "Hello, my name is Sri Mata Amritanandamayi Devi, and I am a Hindu spiritual leader and humanitarian from India." Amma has never said anything like that in her life. So, she just laughed when the documentarian requested her say this sentence. But after a while Amma realized that each section of the documentary was being framed by people from different religions introducing themselves in this manner, and she felt compassion for the director. She didn't want to ruin his plans. So, suddenly Amma said, "This visible form people call 'Amma' or 'Mata Amritanandamayi Devi,' but the indwelling self has no name or address. It is all-pervading."

Through *ātma-anātma viveka*, we have to slowly start to try to view things in this manner. This doesn't mean we renounce all sense of responsibility. The majority of our problems have to be handled to the maximum extent possible, and they should be done so in a *dharmic* manner. We have to maintain our relationships, take care of our health, family and bank balance. We have to perform our duties at work and, as spiritual aspirants, ensure that we do what we can to develop and maintain a disciplined, peaceful and value-enriched mind. But who is the one who has that duty? Even that is not us.

It is a duty of the *ahaṅkāra*—the ego. We are the observer of the *ahaṅkāra*'s efforts, of its successes and failures.

If we contemplate in this manner, we will discover that our reflection creates at least a tiny amount of space between ourselves and our problems. With adherence to this view, that space will gradually expand. From the level of the ego, we still perform our internal and external duties. But from the level of the newly discovered True Self, there is nothing to be done. We are but the witness that is never disturbed—even if the mind is disturbed. Anything we observe—even the mind in utter stress and tension—is not us. We are the witness-consciousness alone.

In this manner, we come to reduce the entire universe to just two things: ourselves—the unexperienceable witness-consciousness—and everything else. Currently, we naturally see everything outside of our body as the world. But in this first stage of Vedānta, we learn to push all of the things we previously indiscriminately considered as part of ourselves out into the world. The body, life energy, mind, intellect, even the sense of doership, etc—all of it is no longer considered me. Just as we have always experienced and understood the world to be separate from us, so too we now learn to experience this body-mind complex as separate from us as well. It is just another part of the cosmos—just a piece of the cosmos to which I, the observer-consciousness, have more intimate access. This view is expressed in several places in the Gītā:

> naiva kiṁcit-karomīti
> yukto manyeta tattvavit |
> paśyañśṛṇvan-spṛśaṇ-jighran
> aśnan-gacchan-svapañśvasan ||
> pralapan-visṛjan-ghṛṇan
> unmiṣan-nimiṣannapi |
> indriyāṇīndriyārtheṣu
> vartanta iti dhārayan ||

> The sage centered in the self should think, "I do nothing at all"—though seeing, hearing, touching, smelling, eating, going, sleeping, breathing, speaking, emptying, holding, opening and closing the eyes—firm in the thought that the senses move among sense objects.[2]

[2] Bhagavad-Gītā, 5.8-9

And:

> tattvavit-tu mahābāho
> guṇa-karma-vibhāgayoḥ |
> guṇā guṇeṣu vartanta
> iti matvā na sajjate ||
>
> However, O mighty-armed one, the knower of the truth regarding the difference between [himself] and the guṇas and between [himself] and *karma*—thinking thus, "The organs rest on the objects of organs"—does not become attached.[3]

In fact, each time we wake up, this is our experience. In dreamless sleep, almost everything experienceable is resolved: The world is gone. Our body and senses are gone. Even our mind and sense of individuality are gone. The only experience is nescience and a timeless blissful peace. But then, we wake up, and one by one, all the observable phenomena return. The first to return is the *ahaṅkāra*—the sense of "I" as a limited individual. Then, even before we open our eyes, our memory comes and reminds

[3] Ibid, 3.28

us of all the relationships we have with other people and the world. Along with that, all of our responsibilities in connection with those relationships return. Suddenly we remember, we have to go to work, feed the dog, take the kids to school, etc. Then we open our eyes, and the world appears. The world we always consider as "other" than me. But if we reflect on this reawakening process, then we can see that all these other layers of experience are also "other than me" as well.

In this regard I am reminded of a joke. Once a man was taken to court for kicking another man. After hearing the plaintiff's side of the case, the judge asked the defendant, "Why did you do it?"

The man answers, "I didn't do it. My leg did it."

The judge looks down at the man and, smiling, says, "Okay, wise guy. Then, the leg can go to jail—with or without you!"

But the defendant didn't blink. He just stood up, unscrewed his fake leg and handed it over to the judge.

Don't take this joke seriously. A true *mahātmā* would never commit a crime or try to wriggle out of responsibilities just because, ultimately, they don't identify with the body. The years of mental and sense discipline required to attain and abide in such a realization have rendered them incapable of harming others by thought, word or deed. Moreover, seeing all beings as one with themselves, they cannot harm even a fly. Amma's attendant, Swamini Srilakshmi Prana, says Amma has even told her to try to carry mosquitos out of the room by hand. Such is the compassion of the true self-realized soul. The story of the one-legged man merely illustrates how, from the *ātma-jñānī*'s perspective, the body, mind and even the sense of agency and of reaping the fruits of our actions are merely part of the world and are not "me."

The more successfully we can do this, the more peaceful we will be—the happier. Because in distancing ourselves from the body, mind and intellect, we are distancing ourselves from literally all of the problems in our life. We cease to be so identified with our actions and their results. Such identification is the cause of all our stress, strain and fear. Thus, if we have set out in search of peace and happiness, then arriving at the True Self from *ātma-anātma viveka* is very helpful. We have already made a lot of progress.

4

Am I Enlightened Yet?

In our journey to peace and happiness, we have taken a tremendous leap forward. We have reduced all of reality—with its infinite parts—to just two elements: *ātmā* and *anātmā*. This pair goes by many different names: self and not-self, spirit and matter, *puruṣa* and *prakṛti*, *sākṣī* and *sākṣyaṁ* [witness and witnessed], *dṛg* and *dṛśyaṁ* [seer and seen], etc. Whatever you call them, ultimately, they are nothing but "me" and "the world." Thus, we have already come a long way.

Is this knowledge what we mean by *ātma-jñānaṁ* though? Is this the end of our journey? We certainly have a new self-definition. We previously thought of ourselves as a mix of consciousness and the body-mind complex. Now, we see that we are only the consciousness. Wasn't our goal a deeper, non-erroneous knowledge of who we are?

In fact, some schools of spiritual thought culminate with this division. However, Advaita Vedānta says this knowledge is woefully incomplete. Because while we have arrived at our true nature as pure consciousness, we still have little to no understanding regarding the nature of consciousness. Moreover, we are still clearly in duality. Reducing the world to two is not reducing it to one. And the spiritual masters like Amma and Ādi Śaṅkarācārya all unequivocally say that the ultimate truth is *advaita*—not two.

Here, we may ask if we really need to know our nature in such detail? Isn't just a general knowledge that "I am pure consciousness" enough? While a general knowledge of the self is helpful, it leaves us wanting. Let us look back to the dialogue between Maitreyī and Yājñavalkya with which we introduced this book. When Maitreyī was offered half of Yājñavalkya's material possessions, she asked her husband:

> yannu ma iyaṁ bhagoḥ sarvā pṛthivī vittena
> pūrṇā syāt syāṁ nvahaṁ tenāmṛtā'ho[3] neti |

> "Lord, even if this earth full of treasure becomes mine, through that will I attain immortality or not?"[1]

Maitreyī understood that if she was not immortal, all the treasures of the earth would become worthless to her upon her death. Even though she was talking about material comforts and pleasures, we can extend this same question to our general discovery that our true nature is pure consciousness: "Is that pure consciousness that I am eternal or not?" This is an important question because while, from the ultimate perspective, I may be untouched by and unconnected to the body, mind, senses and sense objects of the world, if the consciousness is snuffed out with the death of the body, then what is the difference between our outlook and that of the atheist? How will spirituality make me fearless if I am always, consciously or subconsciously, dreading my inevitable destruction? So, at least in terms of my longevity, I would need to know the specific nature of this consciousness.

---

1 Bṛhadāraṇyaka Upaniṣad, 4.5.3

Moreover, I may be pure consciousness, but what about my loved ones? Are they pure consciousness too? If so, is the pure consciousness that is me different from the pure consciousness that is them? And what is this "oneness" that the spiritual masters speak about? All such questions can only be clarified if our general knowledge of our nature is refined into a more detailed and specific knowledge.

At the outset of our journey, we opted to use the *dṛg-dṛśya viveka* model for arriving at our true nature because it did not require knowledge of Vedāntic scriptures or faith in the teachings of the spiritual masters. All we needed was to apply observation and logic. Indeed, that vehicle served us well. However, where we are going next, pure logic will no longer suffice. As the Kaṭha Upaniṣad says:

> naiṣā tarkeṇa matirāpaneyā proktānyenaiva sujñānāya preṣṭha |
>
> Dear one, this knowledge cannot be attained through logic; only when taught by another, established in the truth, it becomes clear knowledge.[2]

---

[2] Kaṭha Upaniṣad, 1.2.9

This doesn't mean that we are going to reject logic. We will keep it as an indispensable tool. However, now, instead of using it only to analyze data gained through the sense organs, we will also use it to analyze data gained from the scriptures.

In Vedānta, we often hear the phrase *śruti-yukti-anubhava* in reference to self-knowledge. It means that we have to use *śruti*—scriptural truths, *yukti*—logic, and *anubhava*—experience. Even though we use all three, we still maintain that *ātma-jñānaṁ* comes only from the scriptural truths. Here, logic and experience take a backseat. We still use logic, but it is primarily to defend the view of the *guru* and scriptures against opposing views and other confusions. While logic and experience cannot reveal the truth to us, neither can they negate it. If they seem to negate it, then we have either misunderstood the teaching, or our logic is flawed, or we have misunderstood our experience. We never reject logic or the value of our objective experience, but we have to understand their limits.

In fact, this is one of the reasons Vedānta should never be studied without a *guru*. Because without a *guru*, any knowledge we arrive at will be limited to sense perception and pure logic. We will lack access to the ultimate truth, which transcends the scope of sensory knowledge and logic. This is something Śaṅkarācārya always stresses. In his introductory commentary to Kena Upaniṣad, Śaṅkarācārya says that this is one of the reasons the scriptures are almost always presented in the form of dialogues between a disciple and *guru*. There, he says, "The teaching is in the form of question and answer between the student and teacher, indeed, for making it easier to understand, since the topic is subtle, and to show that it is cannot be known by independent logic."[3]

In spiritual inquiry, self-analysis rooted in independent logic can be comic-tragic. There is a joke Amma tells that illustrates this. It seems someone offered a donkey a bucket of water and a bucket of whiskey. Observing that the

[3] śiṣyācārya-praśna-prativacana-rūpeṇa kathanaṁ tu sūkṣma-vastu-viṣayatvāt sukha-pratipatti-kāraṇaṁ bhavati | kevala-tarkāgamyatvaṁ ca darśitaṁ bhavati |

donkey would only drink the water, he logically concluded, "Anyone who doesn't drink alcohol is a jackass."

Kidding aside, the fact that logical self-analysis can only take us so far in spiritual life is what Amma means when she says we need a mix of the head and the heart. "The intellect is like a pair of scissors," Amma says. "Its nature is to cut and divide everything. On the other hand, the heart is like a needle that unites objects and people on the single thread of love. When we give more importance to the intellect, life becomes dry. It is love that gives meaning and sweetness to life. Amma is not saying that the intellect is not needed. Both have their own place and importance."

With the scissors of the intellect, we separate ourselves, the pure consciousness, from the external world and all of the other aspects of ourselves that we had mistakenly understood as "I." But that process is not the end. To make our knowledge complete, we require Amma's needle. It is only by using this needle that we will leave behind *dvaita*—duality—and arrive at *advaita*—nonduality, oneness. Why does

Amma say that this requires the heart? Because here we will find that faith in the teachings of the *guru* and scriptures is essential.

5

The Needle & Thread of the Heart

With the intellect, we have reduced who we are to witness-consciousness. However, as we have seen, since this witness-consciousness is ever the subject and never the object, its nature is utterly unknowable through the senses or mind. Everything we know comes to us either directly through our senses of sight and sound, etc, or indirectly through various cognitive functions, such as inference, postulation and comparison, etc.[1] Knowledge gained through indirect means requires data, and that data has to be acquired through the senses. This is why for the next step, we require faith. Because the

---

[1] As per Vedāntic epistemology, there are six *pramāṇams*—valid means of knowledge. These are *pratyakṣa*—sensory perception; *upamāna*—comparison; *anupalabdhi*—nonperception; *anumānam*—inference; *arthāpatti*—postulation; and *śabda*—testimony.

guru and scriptures are our only sources for data regarding the specific nature of the *ātmā*.

Vedānta speaks of two types of knowledge: *pauruṣeya* knowledge and *apauruṣeya* knowledge. In Sanskrit, *puruṣa* means "human being." *Pauruṣeya* means "that which comes from a human being." For example, the fact that "fire is hot" is *pauruṣeya* knowledge—knowledge readily available to all human beings. Any person with properly functioning faculties can learn "fire is hot." That human being can then teach this knowledge to other human beings. Regardless of whether we learn "fire is hot" through our own contact with fire or through someone else's warning, the origin of that knowledge is *pauruṣeya*—of human origin.

On the other hand, take the Law of Karma—the idea that all of our actions not only have gross repercussions based on the physical action, but also a subtle, delayed repercussion, based on our motive. Even though in spirituality, we may refer to this as a "law," it is not a fact like "fire is hot" that can be learned independently by any human being. It can be theorized, but it cannot be known categorically. Thus, the Law of Karma is not *pauruṣeya* knowledge but *apauruṣeya* knowledge—a knowledge that's authority cannot be of human origin. *Apauruṣeya* knowledge has only two sources: revealed scriptures such as the Vedas and human beings who have attained that same knowledge.

The majority of *gurus* have attained their knowledge through a *guru*-disciple lineage. However, the Upaniṣads themselves present examples of self-attained *ātma-jñānīs*, such as Vāmadeva, who attained enlightenment while still in the womb.[2] It is said he studied with a *guru* in his past life, but still had some *karmic* obstacles to his comprehension when he died. Those were removed in the womb itself, and thus he attained enlightenment *in utero*. However, when we trace back the teachings of the Upaniṣads, we find they originate with God himself teaching the first disciple. Thus, if the mind is pure enough, perhaps it's possible to attain *ātma-jñānaṁ* without a *guru*, in that God himself may come and teach you. As for Amma, she says, "From birth itself, Amma knew her true nature and the nature of this world." How

---

2 Aitareya Upaniṣad, 2.1.5

did Amma come to know that? Different people will have different answers. Some believe Amma is an *avatāra* of the Divine Mother; as such, all knowledge is hers alone. Whatever be the reason for Amma's knowledge, she clearly has it, and she is clearly adept at sharing her knowledge with others and clearing their doubts as well.

I remember long back, when some scholars were challenging Amma's opinion regarding an *apauruṣeya* topic—specifically, how could she go against tradition and allow women to perform certain rituals. Since the efficacy of ritual worship itself is *apauruṣeya*, the do's and don'ts regarding it also have to be *apauruṣeya* as well. When they refused to accept Amma's seemingly unorthodox stance, Amma said she did have a valid source for it being acceptable. What was it? Amma said, "Śiva told me it was okay."

Here, we should understand that the relevant question is not "How did Amma attain *ātma-jñānam*?" but "How are we going to attain it?" We have two choices: We can study the scriptures and teachings of our *guru* and have faith in them, or we can scrap tradition and just hope we wake up one fine morning enlightened. But the Upaniṣadic view of people who hope to attain self-knowledge without a *guru* is clear:

> avidyāyām-antare vartamānāḥ svayaṁ dhīrāḥ paṇḍitaṁ manyamānāḥ | jaṅghanyamānāḥ pariyanti mūḍhā andenaiva nīyamānā yathā'ndhāḥ ||
>
> Existing within ignorance and thinking, "We ourselves are intelligent and learned," these repeatedly tormented fools roam about like the blind led by the blind alone.[3]

Maybe we can arrive at the Pythagorean Theorem on our own, but wouldn't it be easier just to study algebra under a math teacher? As Amma says, "Even to learn to tie our shoes, we need someone to teach us. What then to speak of learning the ultimate reality of the universe?"

This topic is always a source of debate. Perhaps the final word can be presented thus: Once in the *āśram*, a heated conversation was underway about whether a *guru* and scriptures

---

[3] Muṇḍaka Upaniṣad, 1.2.8, and (with one word changed) Kaṭha Upaniṣad, 1.2.5

are required. A visitor was adamant that neither were required. As his final evidence, he said, "Buddha and even your Amma did not require a *guru*!" To which one of the *brahmacārīs* responded, "If you think you are a Buddha or an Amma, best of luck."

"What is the true nature of God?" "What is the true nature of the universe?" "What is the true nature of the soul—of 'I'?" "What is the ultimate source of our feelings of limitation, of frustration, of bondage?" "How to overcome such feelings totally and permanently?" "What are the means of doing so?" "What is the goal of human life?" Philosophers can theorize and speculate on such topics, but if we want true knowledge, we have to go to the Upaniṣads, subsidiary texts like the Bhagavad-Gītā and the words of *mahātmās* like Amma. Only they can speak on such topics with conviction and true authority. If purity of mind were enough to know the specific nature of the consciousness that is the self, then why in Kaṭha Upaniṣad, would Naciketā, who is considered a pinnacle of dispassion and mental purity, have wasted one of his boons asking the God of Death about the nature of the self?[4] Mental purity is definitely required, but even if that purity is there, a *guru* is essential to pass down the wisdom.

This is why faith is required for our next step. In fact, faith—*śraddhā*—is enumerated as one of the essential qualities of a Vedānta student.[5] Faith is vital because if we lack faith in the scriptures and the words of the *guru*, we will not consider them valid sources of knowledge. Then our knowledge regarding our true nature will never become firm; we will always suffer doubt. So, firm conviction in the truths of the scriptures is essential. This will never happen

[4] Kaṭha Upaniṣad presents a dialogue between a child disciple, Naciketā, and *guru*, Yama, the God of Death. In the course of the story, Yama gives Naciketā three boons, the third of which Naciketā uses to clarify his doubts regarding the nature of the *ātmā*.

[5] As per the Upaniṣadic tradition, nine qualities are required for Vedāntic study to become fruitful: *viveka, vairāgya, mumukṣutvaṁ, śama, dama, uparama, titikṣā, śraddhā* and *samādhāna*—discernment, dispassion, desire for liberation, mental discipline, sensory discipline, withdrawal, forbearance, faith and concentration. They are never to be abandoned.

if we consider the knowledge they present regarding the self as just "possible theories."

In fact, Amma says, "Everything requires faith, even material science." Ultimate proof does not exist for anything in this world. How can we prove that what we see is real? Can the ears verify it is true? How can we prove what the ears hear is real? Can the eyes verify it? Even so-called "scientific laws" are established on the fact that "they have yet to be unproven." This is because nothing can ever be 100% proven.

Kurt Gödel (1906–1978) was a logician, mathematician and analytic philosopher who is considered one of the most important logicians ever. One of his main contributions is called the Incompleteness Theorems, which he formulated when he was just 25. The essence of the Incompleteness Theorems is that if you have a system of axioms that are consistent—i.e. they are not contradictory—then they are necessarily incomplete. An example is Goldbach's Conjecture, which says: "Every even integer greater than 2 is the sum of two primes." (For example, 3+5=8. Three is a prime. Five is a prime. Eight is an even number.) For small numbers, this can be verified directly. We ourselves can do the math. In 1938, one mathematician decided to verify it himself and got as high as $n \leq 10^5$. With computers it has been verified up to $n \leq 4 \times 101^8$. But the conjecture cannot be proven categorically because, in order to do so, one would have to check infinite numbers. We can assume it is true, but it can never be proven by our direct experience. Gödel, in fact, was a mystic who believed in God. For him, the Incompleteness Theorems were liberating because they meant that ultimately one had to surrender to accepting there will always been an element of unknown mystery in life.

Likewise, material science is also comprised of theories and laws. But none of them are considered sacrosanct. There is always a chance that someone will disprove one. Material science is thus admittedly always a work in progress. While many scientific theories, as scrutinized as they have been, still stand the test of time, others that were prevalent for some time—such as the geocentric model of the universe, etc—were gradually knocked off and replaced with new, more plausible theories. So, as Amma says,

"Faith is not something exclusive to spirituality. We all sit here peacefully because we have faith an earthquake will not happen. We fly because we have faith that the plane will not crash."

I remember once, when we were discussing some higher points of Advaita with Amma, particularly how the True Self is the source from which the entire universe arises, she said, "This is something that cannot be proven. Proof can be given of a scientific solution, and one can prove something which can be perceived by the senses. But the *ātmā* is beyond science or any perception of the senses. You cannot prove it empirically. You experience it within you." Amma then made a very astute point. She said, "But consider that it is the mind that is demanding the evidence. The mind which is *mithyā* [unreal] is demanding that the *satyaṁ* [reality] be proven!"

Thus, faith is essential. It is the job of each spiritual seeker to reflect on the spiritual truths learned from the *guru* and scriptures and weigh them against their logic and experience. If we do this earnestly, gradually we will all begin to appreciate these truths as plausible theories.

Our logic and experience will not negate them. You can try to negate them, but you will fail. Yet, at the same time, you will not be able to prove them either. No one who has understood Vedānta has ever been able to negate it because logic and our experience can never contradict it. Regardless, we cannot take the spiritual truths as just a working theory. If we do, we will never have conviction. Accept them as truth—defectless teachings coming directly from God. Observe the extent to which these truths conform to your logic and experience; beyond that, see how your logic and experience cannot contradict them. Then, through your faith in their source, become convinced that they present the ultimate reality of who you are.

Thus, having faith in the scriptures and *guru* is like gaining a sixth sense. Just as our eyes reveal to us the world of sight and our ears reveal to us the world of sound, the *guru* reveals the world of *apauruṣeya* knowledge—the truth of the self. Thus, the scriptures and *guru* become like a mirror that allows us to see, for the first time, our true face.

6

Our True Face Reflected

The majority of the scriptural statements regarding our true nature are negative. Take for example, this famous line from Muṇḍaka Upaniṣad:

> yat-tad-adreśyam-agrāhyam-agotram-
> avarṇam-acakṣuḥśrotraṁ tad-apāṇi-pādam |
>
> That which is imperceptible, ungraspable, without cause, without quality, has no eyes or ears, no hands or feet.[1]

All the descriptions are in terms of what the True Self is not. Such statements align with our *dṛg-dṛśya viveka* [discrimination between the seer and seen] because the scripture is likewise negating all perceivable things having attributes. As we've already said, if you can see it or hear it or taste, etc, it's not the True Self. Likewise, if you can physically hold it, speak about it, kick it, it's not the True Self. If it has an origin—a

---

[1] Muṇḍaka Upaniṣad, 1.1.6

parent or source of generation—it's not the True Self. Moreover, if it has any sense organs such as eyes or ears, or any organs of actions, such as hands or feet—it's not the True Self.

The scriptures primarily use this method of negtion because they know that once you speak of something in a positive sense, you have invariably limited it to some degree. What is the True Self? It is you—nothing more, nothing less. So, if you want to know what it is, then know who you are. Only then will you know. Thus, the ancient saints and sages thought it was safer to help people understand what the True Self was not, rather than what it was. Thus, *adreśyam-agrāhyam-agotram-avarṇam-acakṣuḥśrotraṁ tad-apāṇi-padam*—"Imperceptible, ungraspable, without cause, without quality, has no eyes or ears, no hands or feet," etc. For, once we say, "The self is 'this' or 'that,'" then we will take it to be an object and set out to find that object. But it is not an object—neither one here, nor one in some other world, nor one found in meditation. It is you—the subject. As the saying goes, "The seeker is the sought." So, *gurus* and scriptures try to avoid positive statements as much as possible.

Recently, a devotee approached Amma during *darśan* and asked her, "Who am I?"

Amma's response was automatic: "You are me."

The devotee smiled, but wanted Amma to tell him more. Shaking his head in disbelief, he said, "Can Amma explain?"

Amma said, "If I explain, it becomes two."

This reminded me of another incident. A few years back during one of Amma's tours in India, a young girl approached Amma from the side during *darśan*. In fact, it was quite crowded, but this child somehow managed to reach the side of Amma's chair. After a while, the little girl told Amma she wanted to ask a question. Amma smiled and nodded her head in encouragement. She then leaned way over to her right so the girl could speak directly into her ear. Everyone watched as Amma listened intently, nodding her head each time she registered one of the little girl's points.

As soon as the little girl finished, Amma told everyone, "She says her father says Amma is Kālī, but her mom says that Amma is their Mother, and she wants to know which one is right!"

Amma laughed good-naturedly with everyone, smiling at the girl's innocence. She then lovingly pinched the girl's cheek and said, "Do you want to know who Amma is?"

The girl's eyes widened, and she nodded.

Amma told her, "If you want to know who *Amma* is, know who *you* are. Then you will know who Amma is."

The self is you. The self is me. Understand who you are and be free.

However, aside from negating what we are not, if we want to gain insight into our true essence in a positive, declarative manner, we find that the *guru* and scriptures finally do reveal that nature. In essence, those positive statements are that the self is *saccidānanda*—pure existence, pure consciousness, pure bliss.

Cit: Pure Consciousness

In *saccidānanda*, the word *cit* means "pure consciousness." In fact, we have already arrived at and discussed this aspect of the self through our *dṛg-dṛśya viveka*. Negating all experienceable phenomena, we arrived at the unnegatable witness—the consciousness that illumines even the blankness in deep sleep. Regardless, we find many statements in the Upaniṣads and Bhagavad-Gītā that directly proclaim this truth: *prajñānaṁ brahma*—"Consciousness is brahman"[2], *tacchubhraṁ jyotiṣām-jyotiṣiḥ*—"It is the pure one; the light of all lights"[3]; *yanmanasā na manute yenāhurmano matam*—"That which man does not comprehend with the mind, that by which, they say, the mind is known"[4]; and *kṣetrajñaṁ cāpi māṁ viddhi sarva-kṣetreṣu bhārata*—"O Bhārata, understand me to be the knower of the body in all bodies."[5]

These are but a very small selection. The Upaniṣads are bedecked with such jewel-like statements revealing our true nature as pure consciousness. The Upaniṣads proclaim with one voice that we are not the body, mind, senses or intellect. We are the witness-consciousness

---

[2] Aitareya Upaniṣad, 3.1.3

[3] Muṇḍaka Upaniṣad, 2.2.9

[4] Kena Upaniṣad, 1.5

[5] Bhagavad-Gītā, 13.2

that stands behind them, ever illumining their presence or absence.

Sat: Pure Existence

Sat means "pure existence." Normally, when someone says, "existence," we immediately ask, "Of what?" Here, however, we are not talking about existence as an attribute of an object, but existence itself—the original entity devoid of any name or form. This is because existence is not an attribute of the self. As we saw through *dṛg-dṛśya viveka*, the self has no attributes. Just as consciousness is not an attribute of the self but the self itself, so too existence is the self. This is the ultimate meaning of *sat*. We find this truth stated in the Upaniṣads in an oft-quoted mantra:

> sad-eva somyedam-agra āsīd-ekam-evādvitīyam |
>
> In the beginning, dear boy, all this, was pure existence alone, one without a second.[6]

However, when we say the self is of the nature of existence, we do also mean that it is eternal. The eternality of the self is proclaimed throughout

[6] Chāndogya Upaniṣad, 6.2.1

the scriptures of Indian spirituality. In fact, this is the very first thing that Kṛṣṇa tells Arjuna about the self.

> na tvevāhaṁ jātu nāsaṁ
> na tvaṁ neme janādhipāḥ |
> na caiva na bhaviṣyāmaḥ
> sarve vayam-ataḥ param ||

> Nor I, nor you, nor any of these ruling princes was ever nonexistent before; nor is it that we shall cease to be in the future.[7]

Probably, Kṛṣṇa told this to Arjuna first because mortality is humankind's fundamental worry. The idea of death as total annihilation is something no one can bear. Without confirmation of our immortality, the fear of impending doom ever nags at us, and sometimes overwhelms us—as Tolstoy famously reflected in his treatise *Confession*: "Is there any meaning in my life that will not be annihilated by the inevitability of death which awaits me?" Or as one comedian joked, "I'm not afraid to die. I just don't want to be there when it happens."

[7] Bhagavad-Gīta, 2.12

Most of the time, people are able to push away that fear, but it lurks deep inside nevertheless, subconsciously informing our thoughts, attitudes and actions. In fact, some psychologists claim that all human activity is primarily an attempt to stick our head in the sand and deny our impending doom. However, if we have confidence in the teachings of the *guru* and scriptures, we can cast off such insecurities because the scriptures tell us right from the start that the *ātmā* is eternal. Just as statements revealing our true nature to be consciousness are found throughout the Upaniṣads, so too are statements revealing our eternality: *nitya*—eternal; *amṛta*—deathless; *ananta*—without end; *śāvata*—timeless*;* *sanātana*—everlasting; *avināśa*—without destruction; *avayava*—without deterioration, etc. Countless such descriptions of the True Self saturate the Vedas.

Amma also knows the majority of people are afraid of death. This is why she regularly reminds everyone at her programs that the death of the body is not the end: "Death is not a complete annihilation. It is only like putting a period at the end of a sentence. Just as we continue writing, life continues." Amma also says, "Death is just like exiting one compartment of a train to enter another. The journey of life continues until we realize our true nature."

When it comes to whether the soul is mortal or immortal, we cannot rely on pure logic. Logic can support our inquiry, but confirmation of this must come from a source beyond the limitations of the human mind. Too often these days, people attack those with faith in life after death as being victims of blind belief, saying that it is all nonsense. In truth, from a purely logical standpoint, the debate is a draw. As is said in Advaita Makaranda:

> na ca svajanma nāśaṁ vā
> draṣṭum-arhati kaścana |
> tau hi prag-uttarābhāva
> carama-prathama-kṣanau |

> And no one can see his own birth or destruction, for these two are [respectively] the last and first moments of prior and posterior nonexistence.[8]

In the above verse, the author is pointing out that firsthand experiential proof of our own mortality

[8] Advaita Makaranda, verse 15, Lakṣmīdhāra Kavi, 15th C.

is unattainable. When it comes to both our own death as well as our own creation, if we want proof, we would have to have been there prior to our birth or after our own demise—both of which are paradoxical impossibilities. The point is that, if we are sticking strictly to the realm of perception and logic, neither can there be votes in favor of the soul's mortality nor can there be votes for its immortality. Left there, Vedānta says, it is at best a stalemate. However, truly, immortality has the advantage because while we all have experienced existence, no one has ever experienced nonexistence. Really speaking, it is nonexistence that is the stuff of fairytales—not life after death. But even if Advaita Makaranda's point merely puts the atheists in check, the Vedāntī has more moves via the wisdom of the *guru* and scriptures, which all uniformly state that the self is immortal.

While our proof for the eternality of the self comes from faith in the *guru* and scriptures, we also have some logical arguments as well. One of these is deftly presented by Śrī Kṛṣṇa in the second chapter of the Bhagavad-Gītā.

dehino'smin-yathā dehe
kaumāraṁ-yauvanaṁ jarā |
tathā dehāntara-prāptiḥ
dhīrastatra na muhyati ||

Just as for the one embodied in the body, are childhood, youth and old age, so too is the attainment of another body. Therefore, the wise one is not deluded.[9]

Having already told Arjuna that the True Self was never born and never dies, Śrī Kṛṣṇa now provides a logical support. It's not proof; proof for the *ātmā*'s eternality is that all of the Upaniṣads and *gurus* emphatically proclaim it so. But it does show that the eternality of the *ātmā* does not transgress logic or our experience. As we said earlier: *śruti-yukti-anubhava*—The scriptural truths, when properly understood, will not violate logic or our experience. Here, Kṛṣṇa says that if we reflect, we will observe that we ourselves—the witness-consciousness—remain unchanged throughout our entire life. As the body moves through infancy, morphs into adulthood, and then begins its decline, the same unobjectified

[9] Bhagavad-Gītā, 2.13

"I" awareness has been there as the unchanging witness of those transformations. So too, it has witnessed the mental changes that have come during these phases as well. In fact, these three stages—childhood, youth and old age—are representative of the three middle phases of six states of change commonly presented in Vedānta: origination, existence, growth, maturation, decline and destruction.[10] If an entity undergoes any one of these six, it must go through the remaining five as well. So, anything that is born must one day die, etc. Certainly, this is true for the body. We have seen countless bodies undergo these six-fold changes. However, Kṛṣṇa says this is not true for the *ātmā*. The *ātmā* is the witness of these six-fold changes. The *ātmā* itself ever remains unchanged. Now, Kṛṣṇa's logical extension is: If we have stood as an unaffected witness during the body's transformation from youth to adulthood to old age—the middle modifications—then, we should also remain an unaffected witness to the body's first and

[10] The *ṣaḍ-bhāva vikāras* [six-fold modifications] are: *jāyate*, *asti*, *vardhate*, *vipariṇāmate*, *apakṣīyate* and *vinaśyati*.

last modifications as well, namely birth and death. Thus, since it is already our experience that we are the unaffected witness of three of these modifications, by logic we should also remain the unaffected witness of the others as well. This is one of the logical supports for the eternality of the self.

In Vedic times, up to at least those of Śaṅkarācārya, the eternality of the soul was all but universally accepted. The debates of Śaṅkarācārya and the other great spiritual thinkers were regarding the nature of the soul, not about whether it existed or not. There was one school of thought, however, known as Cārvāka Darśana[11],

---

[11] According to Hindu mythology, the father of Cārvāka Darśana was Bṛhaspati, the *guru* of the *devatās*. It is said Bṛhaspati did not accept the *darśana* himself, but cooked it up it to mislead the demons, thereby making them easier to destroy. His first disciple was a demon named Cārvāka. Cārvāka literally means "he whose speech is sweet," perhaps a reference to the alluring nature of a philosophy that stresses enjoying as much physical pleasure as possible. Its foundational text, the Bārhaspatya Sūtras have been lost to antiquity. What we know of the philosophy is primarily from treatises of philosophical historians, such as Swāmī

that was completely materialist and rejected the concept of an immortal soul. However, the view was considered so backward that little effort was spent refuting it. If Śaṅkarācārya were writing his commentaries today, perhaps Cārvāka would be one of his main opponents. While the overwhelming majority of the people have faith in God and a continued existence after death, many harbor doubts as well. And of course, many people believe that consciousness is not the stuff of the self, but must somehow be dependent upon the physical body—a product that comes from its assemblage. When this argument is raised in the Brahma Sūtras, Śaṅkarācārya makes a point of elaborately refuting it.[12] Let us briefly look at what Śaṅkarācārya says there.

Equating the *ātmā* with consciousness, Śaṅkarācārya points out that if consciousness were a mere product of the physical body, then it should continue in the dead body as well. The physical body, after all, remains for some time

Vidyāraṇya's Sarva Darśana Saṅgraha, and when Cārvāka viewpoints are presented and negated in the writings of other philosophers.

12 Brahma Sūtra, Aikātmya Adhikaraṇam, 3.3.53-54

after death, and yet no one considers it conscious. Today we can add that even cryogenically frozen bodies are not considered conscious. This points out the logical fallacy of the argument: Because we only experience consciousness via the body, the body must be the source of consciousness.

Śaṅkarācārya then points out the logical fallacy of the opposite side of this argument. Previously, he negated the idea, "Where there is a body there is consciousness." Now he negates the idea that, "Where there is no body, there is no consciousness." He says, just because we don't experience signs of consciousness in a dead body doesn't mean that we can be sure that consciousness is gone. There could be other reasons why consciousness is not expressed in dead bodies. This is a point that Amma frequently makes: "When a lightbulb burns out or a fan stops rotating, it doesn't mean that there is no electricity," she says. "It is still there. It just means the lightbulb or fan have ceased to be proper mediums to manifest that electricity. Consciousness also requires a proper medium to manifest. The *ātmā* is eternal and everywhere. Death occurs not because of the absence of the *ātmā*, but because of the destruction of the instrument known as the body. At the time of death, the body stops being capable of manifesting consciousness. Death marks the breakdown of the instrument—not any imperfection in the *ātmā*." So, Śaṅkarācārya and Amma say that just because we don't experience consciousness in a dead body doesn't mean consciousness is not there. Śaṅkarācārya invokes this argument not to say that, unbeknownst to the living, the individual who availed of the body remains trapped inside the corpse, but to point out that the inability to recognize consciousness in a corpse is not a conclusive argument for its absence.

Śaṅkarācārya then offers a third argument as to why the physical body cannot be the source of consciousness. He says everything we see in this universe—space, wind, fire, water and earth and all of their products—are inert. Therefore, this body, which we can also see and which also is a product of those inert elements, logically also must be inert. As such, how then can it be the source of consciousness?

Yet another argument: Generally, we are able to experience attributes. If someone's body is fat, I experience their fatness. If someone's body has a foul odor, I will experience that too. If this is the case, and consciousness is an attribute of the body, then shouldn't I be able to experience that consciousness as well? Yet, no one has ever experienced someone else's consciousness.

A final argument: To understand this final argument, we have to return to some of the principles we discussed as a part of *dṛg-dṛśya viveka*. There, we said that a perceiver-subject can never perceive itself. The eye with its power of sight can see countless objects, but never itself. Here, Śaṅkarācārya presents a slight modification of this idea. He says that a property of a given substance can never perceive that substance of which it is a property. This means, considering the power of sight a property of the eyes, that property cannot see the eyes; the property of the power of taste cannot taste the tongue. Following this logic, Śaṅkarācārya says, if consciousness were a property of the body, it would not be able to be aware of the body. And yet, of course, we are all conscious of our physical bodies. Therefore, consciousness cannot be a property of the body.

Again, we don't consider any of these arguments as proof that eternal consciousness is the nature of the self or that the self transcends death, etc. The proof is that this is said in the divine scriptures and by the *guru*. But all these arguments can reveal to us the illogical nature of views to the contrary, which all too often act as if they hold exclusive domain on rationality. Thus, faith in the words of the *guru* and scriptures is essential. If we restrict ourselves to logic based on sensory data, we will get nowhere. As Bhartṛhari says:

> yatnenānumito'pyarthaḥ kuśalairanumātṛbhiḥ |
> abhiyuktatarairanyaiḥ anyathaivo papāyate ||
>
> Whatever is logically inferred with great effort by clever logicians is explained otherwise by even cleverer ones.[13]

Therefore, what seems logical from one perspective may seem completely unreasonable from another. As Amma says, "If we want to

[13] Vākyapadīya, 1.34

move through life with firm, unfaltering steps when faced with a crisis, we need to take refuge in God and his path. Without that, life is like a court case in which two lawyers are arguing without a judge. The hearing will go nowhere. If they proceed without a judge, then no ruling is possible." What is the truth? What is the path? What is the nature of this self that I am? We can argue about these things based on logic, but for ultimate conviction, we must embrace the teachings of the *guru* and scriptures.

In the previous quotes of Amma about how death is like a period mark at the end of a sentence or like changing train compartments, etc, Amma was actually speaking about reincarnation. As such, they are statements about the eternality of the soul within the principle of time—how the subtle body survives the death of the physical body and then later takes a new body. They are similar to the Gītā verse:

> vāsāṁsi jīrṇāni yathā vihāya
> navāni gṛhṇāti naro'parāṇi |
> tathā śarīrāṇi vihāya jirṇāni
> anyāni saṁyāti navāni dehī ||

> As a man casting off worn-out garments puts on new ones, so too the embodied one, casting off wornout bodies enters into others that are new.[14]

However, as we said at the beginning of this chapter, the *sat* of *saccidānanda* really is speaking about eternality on another level altogether. It is not an eternality within the principle of time, but an eternality that is the very substratum of the principle of time. Coming to this level, Amma says: "People celebrate their birthdays with big fanfare, but in truth as long as we celebrate our birthday, we are also confirming our death day. The real birthday is the day when we understand that we were never born and will never die. The *ātmā* never dies nor does it take birth. It is like the ocean. The ocean never changes; it remains as the substratum of all the waves that arise in it. What is a wave, after all? It is only water. One wave comes and disappears. Another one comes, and that also disappears. Yet, another one rises up in another place and in another shape. But what are all these? They are nothing but seawater in

[14] Bhagavad-Gītā, 2.22

different shapes and forms. The waves appear and disappear, reappear and disappear again, but the water remains the same; it never changes. So, waves are nothing but the same water in a different shape and in a different place. In the same way, the *paramātmā* manifests as *jīvas* in different forms and different shapes. The forms and shapes appear and disappear, but the essential principle, the substratum—the *ātmā*—remains forever unchanged, like the ocean."

Therefore, when we say the *ātmā* is "pure existence," ultimately, we mean that wherever existence is experienced, that is the self. And where is existence experienced? Everywhere. We all constantly experience existence. It is just that we never experience "pure existence." We cannot experience pure existence because it is who we are, and as we saw in the beginning of the book, "The experiencer-subject can never be the experienced object." Thus, we can only experience ourselves in a reflection. Where do we reflect? We reflect in every object in this universe. How? As the *sat*—the very existence principle that pervades every object.

For example, when we look around the room we see many things: perhaps, a desk, a table, a chair, another person, a cat, a wall, etc. We say, "The desk *is*," "The cat *is*," "The wall *is*," etc. What Vedānta teaches is that these statements, in fact, reveal not a singular experience but a dual experience: the experience of the object and the experience of our self—the pure existence—reflected in that object. The existence aspect is represented by the verb "is."

Thus, you, the *ātmā*, are pure existence. You experience yourself in and through every object—internal and external—in creation. Because wherever an object appears, that object reflects the *ātmā* and the *ātmā* manifests in the object as its existence.

So, what is the world? It is objects plus existence. If you remove the existence, the objects cannot remain because you have taken away their very foundation. On the other hand, if you remove the objects, the existence remains but is no longer manifest. And what is that existence? It is the *ātmā*. And what is the *ātmā*? It is you.

Thus, everywhere you look, you see yourself—your reflection. You are *sat*—the existence principle that is there in and through every experience you have. The one who truly knows the self—the *ātma-jñānī* like Amma—thus knows she is ever experiencing her own self in and though creation. Everywhere we look there is a constant dual experience: the *sat ātmā* plus name and form.

Once when Amma was flying to programs in Australia, a little girl, about five years old, was sitting near her. The child had a coloring book, and Amma asked her if she could color with her. They worked out a deal: The little girl would pick the colors, and Amma would color. In fact, coloring books had been the main way this girl's parents had been keeping her occupied during Amma's programs. Having seen her color so often, one of Amma's disciples regularly had been telling the child, "Just as you are painting those pictures, Amma painted you." So, when the little girl and Amma finished coloring the picture, the child asked Amma, "Did you paint me like that?"

Amma stared at her for a few moments, and then said, "I didn't need to paint you. You know how you look into a mirror and see a second you? You are just a second me—a reflection. Everyone is just a reflection, each and every plant, animal and human being. Even the sticks and stones!"

The child said to Amma, "But you look different than everyone else! You are so much more beautiful!"

Amma kissed her on the forehead and said, "Well, only you see me as different. I see all as the same. You see beauty and ugliness. But for me, there is only beauty because everything is me."

Thus, seeing the pure existence that is our self—the *ātmā*—reflecting everywhere is "next-level eternality." In the past, was that existence principle there? Of course. It is an eternal principle that is there even when the entire universe has resolved: "Nothingness *is*." Time is a relative principle; it requires duality. Only when there are two moments—be they an eon apart or a millisecond—can we speak of time. But even to speak of time requires existence—"time *is*."

It is when we understand that the *ātmā* is the substratum of time that we ascend from understanding the eternality of the self as being within time to "next-level" eternality. Thus, ultimately, the *sat* in *saccidānanda* does not refer to a thing that exists permanently. The *sat* is existence itself—the "*is*-ness" of all impermanent things.

So far, we have been speaking of *sat* in terms of time. But existence is a principle that holds true also in terms of space as well. Just as we say all moments in time are based in pure existence, so too is everything within space: "The house *is* here," "the moon *is* there," "the light *is* everywhere," etc. Every place you can conceive within space, existence is there as well.

Amma never loses sight of how this pure existence is her true nature. Ultimately, Amma is here to uplift us to this perspective. Once, when Amma returned from her World Tour, some of the *āśraṁ* residents who had been missing Amma grumbled, saying, "Amma, you were away for so long. When you are gone that much, we feel like you have left us."

Amma responded, "Where can I go? I can neither go anywhere, nor can I come anywhere." Amma was revealing her identification with the

True Self—the substratum of everything that reflects in each atom as existence.

The all-pervasiveness of the *ātmā* is symbolized in countless stories from India's Purāṇas and Itihāsas, etc. One such story involves Śuka, the son of Vedavyāsa. According to the legend, one day Goddess Pārvatī asked Lord Śiva about the garland of skulls he always wore around his neck. She wanted to know whose skulls they were. Śiva tried to brush off the question, but Pārvatī's curiosity was pricked and she would not be deterred. Finally, Śiva admitted that they belonged to her.

"How can they by my skulls?" she asked.

Lord Śiva explained to her that he loves her so much that each time she dies, he collects her skull from the funeral pyre and puts it around his neck. Then when she is reborn, he finds her and marries her again. Each time she dies, he adds another skull to his garland. Pārvatī was confused. "Why do you get to be immortal, whereas I'm always dying?"

Śiva explained to her that this is because he knows the secret of immortality and she does not. Of course, Pārvatī asked him to teach her.

Being a loving husband, he agreed. But first, he shook his *ḍamaru* drum to scare off any beings within listening distance because only those qualified to hear that secret should hear it. Then, he told Pārvatī that while he told her the secret, she had to periodically say, "Yes, yes," because it was a long tale and he had to know if she started to fall asleep. She agreed, and he began to explain.

As Lord Śiva explained, every few minutes Pārvatī would nod and say, "Yes, yes." But finally, she dozed off. However, Śiva didn't notice. The reason was because in a nearby tree there was a baby parrot inside an egg that was just about to hatch. Listening to Pārvatī say, "Yes, yes," the baby parrot had begun to mimic her as he listened to Lord Śiva's story.

When the story ended, Śiva suddenly noticed that Pārvatī had, in fact, been asleep. He immediately realized that someone other than her had been saying, "Yes, yes." Seeing the freshly hatched parrot, he charged at it with his trident, feeling it must have been unqualified for the knowledge of immortality. The parrot flew as fast as it could, with Śiva fast behind.

The parrot flew here and there but couldn't shake Lord Śiva. Flying at top speed, it turned a corner and came upon the camp of Sage Vedavyāsa and his wife, Piñjalā. At that very moment, Piñjalā, yawned and the parrot flew into her mouth and down into her belly.

Śiva demanded the parrot come out so he could kill it. But Vyāsa explained to him that it was too late now. The parrot was immortal, so Śiva couldn't kill it anyway.

The problem was that the parrot never wanted to come out. It had some wisdom now, and knew that the world was full of bondage and attachment. From within Piñjalā's belly, the parrot said, "If I come out, I will be treated like your son, and we will both experience the pain of bondage." Vyāsa tried to coax it out, but it wouldn't budge. For 12 years the parrot remained in Piñjalā's belly, the whole time growing like an ordinary human child. With a 12-year-old child in her stomach, Piñjalā was in immense pain. So, Vyāsa prayed to Lord Kṛṣṇa, who immediately appeared on the scene. Śrī Kṛṣṇa assured the parrot that it would not suffer attachment and that it would quickly gain *ātma-jñānam* and attain liberation. Pacified, the parrot emerged, the shape and size of a 12-year-old boy. Vyāsa and Piñjalā named him Śuka, meaning "parrot" in Sanskrit.

True to Kṛṣṇa's word, Śuka emerged very detached, and by the age of 16 set off to take *sannyāsa* and do austerities to attain self-knowledge. Vyāsa, on the other hand, had become very attached to his son, and when he found out his son had left, set out to try to find him and dissuade him. However, it was too late. In the depths of his mediation, Śuka had already realized his oneness with the substratum of all the elements and merged into the totality. He was lost to Vyāsa, who as much as he searched, could not find him. Finally, in panic and grief, Vyāsa called out, "Son! Son! Son!" And, as per the story, all of nature—the earth, the wind, the sun, the rivers and even space itself—responded, as if an echo, "*Father... Father... Father....*"

As surreal and fantastical as some Purāṇic stories like this are, they contain the highest truths of spirituality. Whether we believe Śuka really took birth as a boy after flying into Piñjalā's belly, etc, doesn't matter. What matters is that we grasp the truth to which the stories point. As Amma says, "Having extracted the juice from the sugarcane, we can spit out the stock." And in this story, the juice is the truth that, in our ultimate nature, we are the all-pervading pure existence. Vyāsa was searching for his son's limited physical body. But Śuka had realized that he was not the gross physical body, but the *sad-ātmā*—the very essence, the *is*-ness, supporting all bodies, all elements. Thus, Śuka was everywhere. This is what is symbolized by all of Nature responding to Vyāsa when he called out for his son.

It may seem that there is a tinge of sadness to this story, something bittersweet. Śuka has gained the whole universe, but Vyāsa has lost his son. However, in truth Śuka's merging with the universe means he has never left his father. Just as Śuka is the all-pervasive existence, so, too, is Vyāsa. There cannot be two all-pervasives. Thus, ultimately it is not a story of separation, but a story of oneness. There are not many *ātmās*; there is only one *ātmā*. Thus, it is as if a drop of water wept and said to the sea, "Why do I have to be separate from you?" And the sea laughed and said, "What do you mean? We are all the one water."

Amma herself has said about Śuka's merging: "A person who has become one with the supreme consciousness is also one with all of creation. He is no longer just the body. He is the lifeforce shining in and through everything in creation. He is that consciousness that lends its beauty and vitality to everything. He is the *ātmā* that is immanent in everything. This is the meaning of the story."

The truth that our *ātmā* is the only *ātmā*—i.e. that every being in creation since the beginning of time has as its essence the one and the same consciousness—is another specific aspect of our nature that we cannot experience through the senses or gain through logic. It is the truth about ourselves that we learn from the *guru* and scriptures. Once we accept that, we will find that, just as our experience and logic could not produce this nondual knowledge, neither can they negate it. Our reverential faith in the *guru* and scriptures make it a fact for us.

Amma regularly tells us this truth. As we already saw, Amma often says that if we want to know who Amma is, we have to know who we are. The meaning is that the True Self of all is one. As Amma eloquently puts it, "The I in me is you, and the you in you is me."

The Upaniṣads and the Bhagavad-Gītā consistently proclaim this truth of eternal oneness.

> eko devaḥ sarva-bhūteṣu gūḍhaḥ sarvavyāpī sarva-bhūtāntarātmā | karmādhyakṣaḥ sarva-bhūtādhivāsaḥ sākṣī cetā kevalo nirguṇaśca ||
>
> The one divinity, hidden in all beings, the all-pervasive, indwelling *ātmā* of all beings, the supervisor of all *karmas*, the refuge of all beings, the witness, the consciousness principle, nondual, without attributes.[15]

As is said in Īśāvāsya Upaniṣad:

> yasmin-sarvāni-bhūtānyātmaivābhūd-vijānataḥ | tatra ko mohaḥ kaḥ śoka ekatvam-anupaśyataḥ ||
>
> When, to a man of knowledge, all beings become the *ātmā* alone, then what delusion and what sorrow can there be for that seer of oneness?[16]

---

15 Śvetāśvatara Upaniṣad, 6.11

16 Īśāvāsya Upaniṣad, 7

Moreover:

> yadā bhūta-pṛthag-bhāvam
> ekastham-anupaśyati |
> tata eva ca vistāraṁ
> brahma saṁpadyate tadā ||

> When one sees the diversity of beings as being fixed in the one and that their manifestation is from that alone, then he becomes *brahman*.[17]

And in the Gītā, Śrī Kṛṣṇa says:

> sarva-bhūtastham-ātmānaṁ
> sarva-bhūtāni cātmani |
> īkṣate yoga-yuktātmā
> sarvatra sama-darśanaḥ ||
> yo māṁ paśyati sarvatra
> sarvaṁ ca mayi paśyati |
> tasyāhaṁ na praṇaśyāmi
> sa ca me na praṇaśyati |

> The one whose mind is engaged in *yoga* and sees sameness everywhere sees the *ātmā* fixed in all beings and sees all beings in the *ātmā*. Whoever sees me everywhere, and who sees

[17] Bhagavad-Gītā, 13.30

> all things in me, I do not go out of his vision, and he also is not lost to my vision.[18]

These last two verses from the Gītā point out, again, that what we are seeking is a shift in understanding. We have to understand that even though we are seeing diversity, the reality is that there is only one *ātmā* at the heart of all these seemingly diverse beings. This is difficult because the appearance is so confusingly the opposite. To explain this phenomenon, Amma is fond of a particular example—that of the one and only sun reflecting in many pots. Amma says, "Suppose you take 100 pots of water and put them out under the sun. In each pot, you will see a sun—won't you? But that doesn't mean there are 100 different suns. The sun is one; the reflections are many."

This same example is given in the Upaniṣads, using the moon's reflection instead of the sun's:

> eka eva hi bhūtātmā bhūte bhūte vyavasthitaḥ |
> ekadhā bahudhā caiva dṛśyate jalacandravat ||

[18] Ibid, 6.29-30

> Being but one, the *ātmā* of all beings, is present in all beings. Though one, it is seen as many, like the moon in [different jars of] water.[19]

This example is also discussed at length in the Brahma Sūtras[20] as well as in important Vedānta treatises such as Naiṣkarmya Siddhi[21], written by Sureśvarācārya, one of Śaṅkarācārya's four direct disciples. In short, the scriptures and Advaita *jñānīs* all proclaim that there is but one *ātmā* manifesting variously throughout creation as the pure existence that serves as the substratum for every single object we perceive.

Here, our head may start to explode. How can I, this little human being, who cannot even get to work on time, be the all-pervasive principle of pure existence that contains time and space itself—the one True Self manifesting in everything sentient and inert? When we make such a statement, we have to catch ourselves because we have fallen back into ignorance. When the *guru* and scriptures tell us that we are the pure

---

19 Amṛtabindu Upaniṣad, 12

20 Brahma Sūtra, 3.2.18

21 Naiṣkarmya Siddhi, 2.47

existence that serves as the foundation of the entire cosmos, they do not mean we the human being; they mean we the True Self. They mean the witness that remains when we clip away with the scissors of discrimination all the superficial layers of our personality. Remember, we are not this body, not this mind, not this ego. We are the pure witness-consciousness that illumines the body-experience, the mind-experience, the ego-experience. When we have rewritten our self-concept in this manner, then the idea that "I, the pure witness-consciousness, am also pure existence" is not so implausible.

Ānanda: Pure Bliss

Finally, we arrive at the aspect of the self that we have all been waiting for: *ānanda*—bliss. It was for this alone that we started our entire journey—right? The one goal of our entire life—whatever other goals we may pursue—is to be happy, to experience love, peace. All these words are indicated by the word *ānanda*.

Amma and the scriptures tell us that bliss is not an external phenomenon. It is our True Self. Just as we are the one consciousness pervading the entire universe, just as we are the one existence, so too are we the one bliss. Happiness may seem to arise from external objects, but in truth, happiness is our own nature. Some important statements in the Upaniṣads conveying this include:

> yo vai bhūmā tat-sukhaṁ nālpe sukham-asti bhūmaiva sukham |
>
> That which indeed is the infinite [*brahman*]—that is bliss. There is no joy in the finite. The infinite alone is bliss. [22]

And:

> yad-vai tat sukṛtam | raso vai saḥ | rasaṁ hyevāyaṁ labdhvā''nandī bhavati |
>
> That which is known as the self-creator [*brahman*] is verily the source of joy; for one becomes happy by coming in contact with that source of joy.[23]

And:

[22] Chāndogya Upaniṣad, 7.23.1

[23] Taittirīya Upaniṣad, 2.7.1

ānando brahmeti vyajānāt | ānandāddhyeva khalivamāni bhūtāni jāyante | ānandena jātāni jīvanti | ānandaṁ prayantyabhisaṁviśāntīti |

He knew bliss as *brahman*, for from bliss, indeed, all these beings originate. Having been born, they are sustained by bliss; they move towards and merge in bliss.[24]

As said in Amma's quote with which we began this book—"Our lives are meant to be born in love, to live in love and to eventually end in love, but tragically, even though most of us spend our lives in search of love, the majority of us die without ever finding it"—the *ānanda* aspect of the *ātmā* is the most difficult to appreciate. Quite readily we can accept that we always exist. The fact that we are ever conscious is also relatively easy to appreciate. But when the *guru* tells us, "You are of the nature of bliss," we start to think he may be off his rocker. Either that, or he clearly doesn't know our mental state.

Here, again, it is helpful if we take the example of the mirror. Remember, being the subject, we can never directly experience ourselves. We only

[24] Ibid, 3.6.1

experience our self indirectly, as reflected in the surrounding universe—both in the external universe of the world as well as in the internal universe of the body-mind complex. As explained earlier, our existence aspect reflects everywhere and anywhere. Anywhere something "is"—"the floor *is*," "the wall *is*," "the boy *is*," the mind *is*," etc—that "is" is a reflection of the *ātmā*. Any object—no matter how gross—reflects our "is-ness."

To reflect our consciousness aspect, however, the matter must be subtle. The gross elements—space, wind, fire, water and earth or their combinations like tables, chairs, buildings—are unable to reflect consciousness. They can reflect the *sat* aspect of the *ātmā*, but not its *cit* aspect. The mind, however, can and does reflect consciousness. The mind of every sentient being is able to reflect consciousness to some degree—be it of a cockroach, a bird, a dog, a whale or a human being. (Even plants, though immobile, have a nervous system of sorts, allowing them to faintly reflect consciousness as well.) Thus, consciousness reflects in minds—not in the gross insentient objects of the world. Śrī

Śaṅkarācārya puts this very succinctly in his Advaitic treatise Ātmabodha:

> sadā sarvagato'pyātmā
> na sarvatra avabhāsate |
> buddhāvevāvabhāseta
> svacchesu pratibimbavat ||

> Though all-pervading, the *ātmā* does not shine in everything. It is manifest only in the mind, like a reflection in something pure.[25]

The more refined the mind, the brighter consciousness reflects. Thus, we may use expressions like, "He is of a higher consciousness" or "he elevated his consciousness" or "through evolution, lifeforms evolved consciousness," but in all such expressions what "evolves," "heightens," or "elevates," etc, is not consciousness but the mind's ability to reflect a finite, localized semblance of the all-pervading consciousness aspect of the *ātmā*.

While existence reflects in every aspect of creation, and while consciousness reflects only in the subset of creation called "mind," bliss

[25] Ātmabodha, 17

reflects in an even smaller subset: the tranquil mind. This is why we see bliss so tangibly in those rare *mahātmās* like Amma. Amma's mind is so peaceful that the bliss of the self ever radiates within it. Likewise, there are times when our minds also become still and peaceful, and during those times we also experience bliss. We can still the mind to various degrees in meditation and experience the *ātmā*'s reflection in our mind as bliss. In deep sleep, the mind also resolves into stillness; thus, we all know sleep to be most blissful. The mind can also be artificially stilled through drugs. It can also be temporarily stilled through fulfilling our desires. The problem with stilling the mind through drugs and fulfilling desires is that, when the effects wear off, the mind becomes even more agitated than it was prior to its artificial stilling. Thus, caught in a vicious cycle, many people end up destroying themselves and their families in vain hope of attaining something that is, in fact, their true nature.

While the mind's ability to reflect our blissful nature depends upon the mind's condition, a basic level of bliss is almost always reflected. In fact, we take this level for granted. Only when it disappears or shrinks to negligible levels do we realize we lost it. Amma often says, "We only realize we have a head when we have a headache." Similarly, we only realize that we are always experiencing a basic level of reflected bliss when that basic reflection fades away. During clinical depression and withdrawal from addictive drugs, the mind can become like that. This basic level of bliss is referenced in Bṛhadāraṇyaka Upaniṣad: *etasyaivānandasyānyāni bhūtāni mātrām-upajīvanti*—"Other beings live on a particle of this bliss alone."[26]

We experience this truth regularly. We think we are unhappy in a given situation. We complain left and right. Then what happens? The problem gets worse. Suddenly, we think, "I'd give anything to get back to that old level of unhappiness." Means, some small degree of *ānanda* is almost always reflecting.

There is a story like this. A couple comes to a *guru* and tells him they are always fighting and are unhappy. The *guru* tells them to get three dogs and to let them live in the house with them.

[26] Bṛhadāraṇyaka Upaniṣad, 4.3.32

"Whatever you do, don't let them out," he says. "Come back in a week." The couple does so.

"So, how is it?" the *guru* asks. "Horrible," they say. The whole house smells of dog and dog mess. The *guru* nods and says, "Okay, get eight cats. Never let them out. Come back in a week." The husband and wife look at each other hesitantly, but go ahead with the plan.

Seven days later they return. "So?" inquires the *guru*.

"It's a nightmare!" they say. "Dogs chasing the cats; cats hissing and fighting each other. The house smells wretched."

The *guru* nods again and says, "Okay. Now get 10 geese. Keep them in the house. See me in one week."

The couple returns a week later. They look horrible. The wife's face is all puffed up. The man's arm is in a sling. Their clothes are filthy. They look like they haven't slept. The *guru* says, "Well?"

The couple breaks down crying, "It's a hell. Feathers everywhere! Two dead geese. I slipped in goose poop and broke my arm. It seems my wife's allergic to cats. She can barely breathe. The whole house is one big, putrid chaos!"

The *guru* says, "Okay. Get rid of all the animals. Come see me in one week."

A week later, the couple returns. They are holding hands, smiling, beaming—the picture of matrimonial harmony. They fall at the *guru*'s feet and praise him for his ability to work miracles.

The teaching of the story is that some degree of happiness reflects in the mind, even in so-called "unhappiness." If we want the mind to reflect more bliss, there is only one sustainable means: making it more tranquil through meditation and reducing our likes and dislikes.

I remember once, long ago, when I was driving Amma and the other *brahmacārīs* in a van, an elderly devotee sitting in the seat next to me kept looking at Amma's reflection in the rearview mirror. He remarked very innocently, like a child, "I can see Amma's image in the mirror." When he said this, Amma laughed and said, "You will be able to see God everywhere when the mind is cleansed of all its impurities and made into a clear mirror."

Amma was revealing this truth. The mind is like a mirror. The more we polish that mind, the clearer the bliss of our True Self will reflect for us to experience. The more we neglect that mirror—falling into selfishness, negative thought patterns and indiscipline—the cloudier the mirror becomes. However, regardless of how polished or dirty the mirror is, the reality of the self remains the same. It is *saccidānanda*—existence, consciousness, bliss.

There is a technique that Amma has instructed many people to try that is aimed at helping us appreciate that wherever bliss is appears—in our mind or in the mind of other creatures—it, in fact, is our own reflection, a reflection of the True Self. Sometimes people will tell Amma that they are sad because they wish they could spend more time near Amma. They see other people going for *darśan* or speaking with Amma, and they get jealous of the bliss they see those people experiencing. In response, Amma often will tell them, "When you see someone enjoying being with Amma, then you should try to see that person as yourself."

I feel many people take this instruction lightly, as if Amma is merely placating them. In truth, Amma is initiating them into a profound Advaitic practice—one wherein we remind ourselves that we—the True Self—are the one source of all bliss experienced in creation, and that everywhere in the world bliss is experienced is our own reflection.

It is when we understand these three reflections of the self that we begin to appreciate that the self is all-pervasive—that wherever we look, there we are. Whenever we see someone smile or laugh, we should recognize, "That bliss shining in him is a reflection of me, the one True Self." Whenever we see another living creature, we should understand, "Just as I am conscious, it is also conscious; that consciousness is a reflection of me, the one True Self." Moreover, wherever we see anything at all: "The '*is*-ness' supporting that object—that is a reflection of me, the one True Self." There is a beautiful verse in a Vedāntic treatise that wonderfully expresses this ultimate vision:

asti bhāti priyaṁ rūpaṁ
nāma-cetyaṁśa-pañcakam |

ādya-trayaṁ brahma-rūpaṁ
jagad-rūpaṁ tato dvayam ||

Existence, consciousness, bliss, form and name—these are the five parts. The first three are of the nature of *brahman*, and the next two, the nature of the world.[27]

In the verse, the terminology is slightly different from what we have been using. There, existence is referred to as *asti*; consciousness as *bhāti*; and bliss as *priyam*. Those three—wherever I experience them—belong to me—*brahman*, the True Self. The only other two things we experience are mere name and form, which is the world.

Thus, in the vision of Amma and the scriptures, everywhere we see nothing but our own self. In that Vedāntic vision, our thinking should gradually become, "In some places, like in a log of wood or buildings, I reflect as existence. In some places, such as in birds and other animals and people, I reflect as existence and consciousness. And in some other places—such as the person laughing at

[27] Dṛg-Dṛśya Viveka, 20

a joke or as birds blissfully chirping or in a dog smilingly wagging its tale—I reflect as existence-consciousness-bliss. Regardless, of when and where and to what extent I reflect, I am not the reflection. Let the reflections come, let them go, I am the eternal original that never comes or goes—the one self-effulgent subject, reflecting diversely in infinite names and forms."

This is Amma's vision and the vision up to which she is trying to lift us.

I remember one particular time when Amma revealed this vision of hers. It was during a question-and-answer session in Seattle. A devotee said to Amma, "Amma, when I look into your eyes, I feel like I can see the entire universe in them." She then asked Amma why her eyes were so beautiful and, more pointedly, had Amma herself ever contemplated the beauty of her own eyes.

Amma responded, "Amma sees her own eyes through the eyes of her children."

In fact, this statement is like a *sūtra*. In its brevity, the entirety of spirituality can be unfolded. Amma was saying that while it's true, she cannot physically see her own eyes—because, as we have said repeatedly, the seer cannot be the seen—regardless, in her supreme wisdom, Amma knows that it is she alone who is reflecting variously in all aspects of creation. The seer cannot be the seen, but the seen is a reflection of the seer.

This is the vision by which we attain true oneness. This is the vision by which we know that we are the essential substratum of every mountain, lake, river and ocean, of every star and breeze, even of all of space itself. It is the vision by which we finally understand, as Amma says, that "the I in me is you, and the you in you is me." It is the vision by which we know every laugh and every smile is a reflection of the bliss that is our True Self.

It is only in this vision that we finally become free. For when we truly understand that nothing exists other than we ourselves and our reflection, where is the scope for fear in life? Who is there to hate or to be angry with? What is there to seek or run from? We have understood that everything is we ourselves and we ourselves alone. Then, we understand that all the statements in the Upaniṣads about *brahman* or the *ātmā* or "that" are not talking about something remote and unknown; they are talking about we ourselves:

> The fire is simply that; the sun is that; the wind is that; and the moon is also that! The bright one is simply that; *brahman* is that; the waters are that; and Prajāpati is that! You are a woman; you are a man; you are a boy or also a girl. As an old man, you totter along with a walking stick. As you are born, you turn your face in every direction. You are the dark-blue bird, the green one with red eyes, the raincloud, the seasons, and the ocean. You live as one without a beginning because of your pervasiveness, you, from whom all things have been born.[28]

Originally, through our process of *dṛg-dṛśya viveka,* we discriminated away everything we experience as necessarily "not me." The world with all of its objects is an experienced object. Therefore, it cannot be me, the experiencer-subject. This body and its organs of action and

28 Śvetāśvatara Upaniṣad, 4.2-4

knowledge also are experienced; therefore, not me. So too the energy in the body—not me. Likewise, all of our thoughts, emotions, ideas, concepts; even our sense of being a thinker, of being an agent of action and of being an experiencer; even all the peace and happiness I experience. Since I am aware of all of these things and phenomena, they are all objects, and therefore none of them can be me. However, now, we understand, "Wait, while all of these are indeed objects and not the original me, at the same time, they are still reflections of me. I am the *saccidānanda*—the existence-consciousness-bliss pervading everywhere. Thus, all that is, regardless of which dimension of reality, is nothing but me—infinite reflections of me.

This is the ultimate knowledge—the worldview in which Amma eternally abides—an ecstasy wherein we see our own eternal, blissful self, reflected everywhere:

> mayyeva sakalaṁ jātaṁ mayi sarvaṁ pratiṣṭhitam
> | mayi sarvaṁ layaṁ yāti tad-brahmādvayam-
> asmyaham ||

In me alone, everything has arisen. In me alone all is sustained. Back into me everything resolves. I am that infinite pure consciousness, other than which nothing else exists. [29]

[29] Kaivalya Upaniṣad, 19

7

Living Vedānta

"Enlightenment to me is like peanuts." This is something Amma occasionally says. When we first hear it, we are shocked. How can the most precious and valuable thing in creation—the only true goal of human life—be, in Amma's eyes, like something you can get on any Indian street corner for just 20 rupees?

In fact, this is Amma's way of stating that, for her, the true divine nature of this world, of herself, of God—the essential oneness of all of us—is so inherently obvious as if to be commonplace. It is like the knowledge, "The sun is yellow" or "water is wet." Moreover, when Amma says, "Enlightenment to me is like peanuts," she is also pointing to the ultimate simplicity of the spiritual teaching. As we have seen throughout this book, the Advaitic view in itself is not complicated. It is wondrous, and, initially, aspects of it may seem counterintuitive, but it is something that most anyone should eventually be able to understand: You are not the body and mind. You cannot be them because you observe them. Therefore, you are the totally unobjectifiable witness-consciousness. The nature of that unknowable "you" is that it is the one eternal substratum of all of creation. All of creation arises from it, is sustained in it and resolves back into it at the end of a cycle of creation. Everywhere you experience existence, consciousness or bliss—that is you alone reflected in this creation, which is eternally arising from you like a mirage. This knowledge itself—as incredible as it may seem to us—is simple. To Amma, it is like peanuts.

Self-knowledge is precious, no doubt. But the real value—for us and for the world—comes when we are able to fully absorb that knowledge, to have it saturate our subconscious mind and translate it into action. Thus, Amma's emphasis has always been on *jñāna-niṣṭhā*, not just *jñānam*. For Amma, without *niṣṭhā*, *jñānam* has only limited value. It's like getting the joke, but never being overcome with laughter.

Niṣṭhā is the state of being firm in knowledge, unwavering, fixed. One becomes *niṣṭha* when the knowledge doesn't remain only on the surface but has saturated the subconscious mind. When this happens, our thoughts, words and actions will always be in alignment with our Vedāntic knowledge. That is what makes Amma so special. Countless people have understood Vedānta and have reaped tremendous emotional benefit from its ultimate teaching, but the extent to which Amma is one with that teaching and the extent to which it radiates through her every thought, word and deed is all but unprecedented in the annals of spirituality.

For Amma, the basic benchmarks of *jñāna-niṣṭhā* are two: mental equanimity and compassion. Does our knowledge that we are not the body or mind translate into mental equanimity in the face of success and failure? Of praise and criticism? Does our knowledge of our oneness with all beings translate into kindness and compassionate service to them? This is what Amma calls "Living Vedānta." And this is the central message of Amma's life. This is where she places value.

The following is the example Amma consistently uses to show how *ātma-jñānaṁ*, when properly assimilated, should manifest as compassion for others. Amma says, "Suppose the left hand is injured. Does the right hand say, 'Oh, that's the left hand; it has nothing to do with me?' No, the right hand immediately presses and soothes the left hand, and applies medicine if needed. This is because it does not see the left hand as different from itself. If we have true spiritual understanding, this is how we will react to the suffering of all beings."

Amma's entire life is a manifestation of this principle in action. A few years back a journalist said to Amma, "You spend so much time, night and day, helping other people, drying their tears and answering their questions. What about you? Don't you take any time for yourself? Amma's response was touching, "I see no difference. *Their* time is *my* time."

This is the vision of a true *ātma-jñānī* like Amma. Kṛṣṇa expresses the same sentiment in the Gītā when he says:

> ātmaupamyena sarvatra
> samaṁ paśyati yo'rjuna |
> sukhaṁ vā yadi vā duḥkhaṁ
> sa yogī paramo mataḥ ||

> O Arjuna, one who views happiness and sorrow everywhere [in all beings] by applying the same standard he would apply to himself, that yogī is considered supreme.[1]

When it comes to showing how the proper assimilation of *ātma-jñānaṁ* leads to mental equanimity, Amma gives another example. Generally, when tragedies befall others, we remain detached. Amma says, if we have assimilated self-knowledge, we will naturally demonstrate that same degree of detachment when problems come our way as well. She says that currently when our neighbors lose a loved one or suffer hardships, we can easily provide them with sage Vedāntic advice. But if the same tragedies were to befall us, we would find that we are the ones crying. When we truly assimilate consciousness as our nature, we will identify with the witness. Then we will view everything that happens to our body-mind complex with the same detachment as if it were happening to someone else. Amma says, "The principle behind being a witness is the attitude of seeing nothing as our own. This

[1] Bhagavad-Gītā, 6.32

is because when we view both the good and the bad without preconceived notions, identifying with pure awareness, then our actions and their results cannot bind us. The culmination of the witness state is when our mind becomes like a mirror. A mirror never says, 'Oh, how beautiful!' or '*Eww!* How repulsive. It's so ugly!' It just silently reflects everything that comes before it."

Once, an *āśraṁ* resident asked Amma what was the value in assimilating the truth "I am consciousness"? After a while Amma began telling him about a series of mistakes another *āśraṁ* resident had made. He listened attentively as Amma enumerated this person's errors, agreeing with her as she spoke, even smiling. Suddenly Amma stopped. She said, "You know I'm not talking about someone else—don't you? I'm talking about you. People told me you did these things." The smile immediately vanished from his face.

Amma then said, "You see the value of being able to remain a witness? When you thought these mistakes were made by someone else, my words didn't bother you. You remained a witness and smiled at everything. But when you realized that you were being blamed, your cheerfulness vanished. The state of being a witness is the ability to stand back and watch everything with a smile, without getting attached to any situation or forming any sense of ownership."

Thus, Amma says when we feel anger towards someone, we should try to think, "I am not the body; I am the pure consciousness. I am not what that person said I am, so why should I feel anger? Even he is not the body, but pure consciousness. So, with whom am I getting angry?"

This is where the value of self-knowledge comes—when we not only understand that we are not the body-mind complex, but when we can also stand firm in that knowledge in times of adversity and not react when this body-mind complex is criticized. Similarly, the value of self-knowledge manifests when we understand our oneness with all creatures not only intellectually, but when we love and serve them as readily as we naturally love and serve ourselves.

In 2004, after the Indian Ocean Tsunami, the entire the *āśram* and the villages around it were completely flooded. Amma spent the entire day waist deep in the floodwaters evacuating people—*āśraṁ* residents, visitors and villagers. In the evening, she was the last to cross over to the mainland. At that time, I asked Amma how she was doing. Amma said, "No matter what is happening outside, inside, I am always serene." That is the sign of *jñāna-niṣṭhā*—inner serenity even in the face of a tsunami.

Similarly, back in the early days of the *āśram*, a man named Dattan, who was a leper, would come for *darśan*. Amma would clean his wounds with her bare hands and tongue, sometimes even sucking puss out from his sores. At that time, I also asked Amma, "Amma, how can you do that? Doesn't it revolt you?" Amma said, "Son, do you feel aversion when you care for a wound on your own arm? I don't view his body as in anyway separate from me." Such tender, compassionate service to those in need, without concern for yourself—that is *jñāna-niṣṭhā*.

Unlike regular people, the *avatāra* chooses the circumstances of her life: Where she will be born, where she will live, what she will do, etc. And with the resolve to teach this "Living

Vedānta," Amma has crafted the perfect means in her *darśan*.

Once to illustrate this, a *brahmacārī* shared the following imaginary story about Amma. He said, it is as if before this birth Devī was seated in the heavens, and she began to contemplate life on earth. She asked her celestial companions—her *śaktis*—"Where should I be born?" And thinking of a nice vacation with her, they said, "*Hmm...* Kerala! It's so beautiful. It's God's Own Country!"

And Devī said, "Let it be so."

Then Devī asked, "To whom should I be born?"

And the *śaktis* thought, "Well, it should be somewhere remote so that not too many people come and bother us." So, they said: "There is a *dharmic* couple who live between the backwaters and the Arabian Sea. They are very pious." (They left off the part about there not being a bridge!)

Again, Devī said, "Let it be so."

Then Devī asked, "But what shall I do there?"

And the *śaktis* said, "You can instruct people in *dharma* and teach them their divine nature."

"Let it be so," said Devī.

"But how should I teach them that?"

And the *śaktis* all fell silent. For the ability to speak about that truth—which is beyond words and the mind, which can never even be objectified—that is a wonder.

But eventually one of the *śaktis*—who was known to be a bit of a comedian—joked, "Well, maybe you can just hug them."

The other *śaktis* were all confused. "Hug them?"

The comedian *śakti* laughed and said, "Yeah, you know, like merging of the *jīvātmā* and *paramātmā*."

It was meant to be a joke, but Devī's eyes lit up. "Yes! Yes! I will hug them."

The *śaktis* got a little nervous. Something about that look in Devī's eyes...

Devī said, "First, there will be just a few. And I will listen to their problems and dry their tears and hug them and do everything I can for them. And from this, people will see that it's possible to care for someone as much as you care for your own self. But then there will be more, hundreds, and I will hug them and show them true compassion as well."

The *śaktis* were getting more nervous. They didn't like the sound of this at all. But Devī was getting more and more excited.

"And then there will be thousands, and I will hug them and show them my love and compassion too. And people will think, 'How can she do that? It's taking hours and hours! She's not stopping for anything! She doesn't take time for herself! Her whole life is just drying these peoples' tears and consoling them! Doesn't she need to rest? How can she tolerate it? How does she keep on smiling?'

"But I will not stop.

"And then the thousands will turn into millions. And some of them will throw flowers, and some of them will throw stones, but I will love them all the same. I will show every single one the compassion they are so desperately thirsting for. And some will mock me and chide me. Some will betray me, but I will still show them nothing but love.

"And then tens of millions will come. And no one will believe it. They will say, 'How can she do that? Her body must be breaking!' And that body I take will be breaking. But I will still be smiling. I will cheer them on in their success and dry their tears in their sorrow. I will show them—I will show the entire world—what Vedānta is really about. What it really means and looks like when someone knows they are God and that the entire universe is their child."

And the *śaktis* then said, "Please, Devī, don't do that! Do you know how painful it will be? The people will be so ignorant. They will just want more and more and more of you. They will never let you rest with their problems and troubles and questions and letters. And in spite of you teaching them and showing them the truth, the majority won't even understand! We can't even bear to hear it! We don't want to see you in such pain."

But even as they were saying this, the bright red of Devī's *sāri* was already starting to fade to white. Likewise, Devī's long-flowing black hair was already beginning to gather itself up into a bun. And then, before their eyes, Devī's slender body began to become just a little plump, so as to be perfect for hugging.

And Devī, heard the *śaktis* say, "Oh, Devī, this idea you have is too much for us to bear—too wondrous. Please, don't do it!"

And Devī said, "No, it's perfect. That's exactly how I want it to be."

Once we have understood the Vedāntic teaching, it is our duty to strive to put that teaching into practice as much as possible. The extent to which Amma lives Vedānta may be impossible for us. Yet, we should keep her perfection as a polestar towards which we constantly direct the journey of our life. This means that we should understand how all of the divine qualities we see in Amma are reflections of the Vedāntic teaching. Appreciating that, we must stand firm in our knowledge and emulate them. We must emulate Amma's patience, her self-control, her compassion, her detachment from the hardships she faces and from the pains of her body, her freedom from likes and dislikes, the alacrity with which she sacrifices herself for others and rushes forward to help them. All of it. As Śaṅkarācārya says in his commentary on the second chapter of the Bhagavad-Gītā, "For in all the spiritual scriptures, whatever are the characteristics of the enlightened person are themselves presented as the spiritual practices for the spiritual aspirant."[2] These efforts of ours, when combined with our Vedāntic understanding, gradually take us from *jñānaṁ* to *jñāna-niṣṭhā*.

From the ultimate perspective, the mind is also a *māyā*. Means, if we are not the mind, what do we care if it is suffering? Some peak Vedāntic texts take this position. Ultimately, they are correct. Moreover, the mind will always fluctuate to some degree. It is matter, just like the body. Just because we have attained Vedāntic knowledge, does not mean our arm will not bruise if someone punches it. Similarly, emotions are the mind's nature. To some extent, they will be there. Ultimately, liberation is not in controlling the mind; it is the understanding "I am not the mind." We are not *avatāras* like Amma. Her degree of *niṣṭhā* should guide us forward, but it may be millennia before the world sees a mind express such *niṣṭhā* again. Regardless, it is our

[2] Bhagavad-Gītā, 2.55: sarvatra eva hi adhyātma-śāstre kṛtārtha-lakṣaṇāni yāni tāni eva sādhānani upadiśyante yatna-sādhyātvāt.

dharma to strive constantly to improve and discipline our mind—to align our mind with our Vedāntic knowledge. At the same time, we should never forget that, "Regardless of the condition of my mind, the mind and its thoughts and emotions really have no effect on me, the witness-consciousness."

These are not contradictions. Let us understand we are not the mind, but yet ever strive to improve the mind. Just because we may understand Advaita Vedānta, doesn't mean we should ever abandon our mental disciplines. We should spend time daily in meditation, do *arcana*, chant our *mantra*, engage in *seva*. After all, though the ultimate teaching of Advaita is "I am not the mind but pure existence-consciousness-bliss," if we want to enjoy that bliss—if we want to taste the *advaita-makaranda*, the nondual honey that we are—then we have only one means to do so: through its reflection in the mind. Thus, we should not stop refining and maintaining our mind, even though the mind and what is reflected in it ultimately are not the real me. It is just that, having understood the ultimate *advaitic* teachings of the *guru* and scriptures, we no longer do such actions in order to attain liberation. Our thinking becomes: "I am free. I always have been, always will be. But this mind has various problems. Let me work on correcting them. That has nothing to do with my true nature. Yet, let this be a lifelong project—to make this mind as good and as refined and as harmonious with the rest of creation as possible. This way I can be more kind and loving. This way the love inside me will not be 'trapped like honey inside a rock,' as Amma says, but will be shared freely with all."

Here, Vedānta stresses the importance of *nididhyāsanam*. First, we listen and we learn Vedānta from the *guru—śravaṇam*. Then we clear any doubts that may arise by reflecting and asking questions: *mananam*. Then, once the knowledge is complete and clear, if we want to attain the state of *niṣṭhā*—if we want the knowledge to saturate our mind as it does Amma's—then we must intentionally dwell in that knowledge. This is called *nididhyāsanam*. Knowledge that has yet to saturate the subconscious mind is not much different from knowledge that is still in the book.

Amma says, "We may hear countless times that we are not the body, mind or intellect—that we are the embodiments of bliss. But we forget this when we encounter even trivial problems. Constant practice is therefore essential if we want to be strong in the face of difficulties. We need to train the mind to remain in that awareness continuously. The mind should be trained to push away all obstacles from our path with the conviction that we are not lambs but lion cubs." Here, Amma is referring to *nididhyāsanam*.

In America in the 1960s, there was a very popular TV program called *The Andy Griffith Show*. It centered around a small-town country sheriff and his egoistic, impetuous deputy, played by the comic actor Don Knotts. In one episode, the deputy starts studying judo. He asks the sheriff—who is much bigger than he is—if he can demonstrate some moves for him. He tells the sheriff to come at him. The problem is that the deputy can only remember and demonstrate his counterattacks when the sheriff comes at him both in slow motion and exactly as per the attack in the book. If the sheriff rushes at the deputy full speed or in manner different than presented in the book, the deputy invariably ends up pinned to the ground. Just as judo is only helpful if it saturates our subconscious, so, too, it is with Vedānta. That is *niṣṭhā*. That is where it gets its real value. One may technically know judo moves, but if they have not practiced them enough, the moves will not readily be at their disposal. Similarly, until it becomes part and parcel of how we think, walk and talk, we also have to "practice Vedānta."

Amma often laments, "People want a discount. So, I give discounts. But when you get too much of a discount, the quality comes down." What Amma means is that she will never force us. If we don't want to do meditation, *arcana*, *seva*, etc, Amma is not going to reject us. She will not throw us out of the *darśan* line. She will continue to show us her love and compassion. She will allow us that "discount." But who loses out through that discount? The quality of the fruit we get from our spiritual understanding is what gets lost; its quality decreases in direct proportion to the discount we take.

Our mind really needs a certain degree of refinement for Vedāntic knowledge to bear fruit. That is why, traditionally, it is said that before entering Vedānta, one should cultivate at least some degree of *sādhana-catuṣṭaya saṁpatti*—literally, the wealth that comes from four spiritual practices.[3] That is why we need discernment, detachment and thirst for the goal. We need mental and sense discipline. We need a peaceful mind that is capable of concentration. We need a degree of introversion and faith in the teachings of the *guru* and scriptures. In fact, if we have *sādhana-catuṣṭaya saṁpatti* at a high level, *ātma-jñānaṁ* dawns very quickly when taught by the *guru*, and *niṣṭhā* follows almost as a matter of course.

But how do we attain these? They come through living a life of values—a life of kindness and truthfulness, patience, compassion, and humility.

[3] In fact, as mentioned earlier, "four" spiritual practices really means "nine," because one of the four is actually six. Thus: are *viveka, vairāgya, mumukṣutvaṁ* and *śāmādi-ṣatka saṁpattiḥ* (*śama, dama, uparama, titikṣā, śraddhā* and *samādhāna*)—discernment, dispassion, desire for liberation and the six-fold wealth beginning with mental discipline: mental discipline, sensory discipline, withdrawal, forbearance, faith and concentration. They are never to be abandoned.

They come through practicing *karma-yoga* and a disciplined meditation practice. Perhaps we can understand Vedānta without doing these things and without gaining *sādhana-catuṣṭaya saṁpatti*. After all, we can even study Vedānta at universities these days. However, the students are not attaining enlightenment and neither is their professor. Why? They have gotten the knowledge at the discount of skipping *sādhana-catuṣṭaya saṁpatti*. We should make sure we don't get self-knowledge with the same discount. If we understand Vedānta but still don't feel we are gaining its emotional benefit, then the problem lies in our lack of mental refinement. If that is the case, then we must put in more effort to develop *sādhana-catuṣṭaya saṁpatti*. In fact, even *sannyāsīs* should never renounce the discipline of continuing to refine *sādhana-catuṣṭaya saṁpatti*.

The best way to ensure we are ever diligent regarding *sādhana-catuṣṭaya saṁpatti* is to maintain a close and devoted relationship with a *sadguru* like Amma. Our devotional bond with the *guru* is the best way to remain steadfast in such disciplines. Before the luminosity of Amma's perfection, the defects of our mind are laid bare. Confronted with those defects, the combination of *guru*'s encouragement and our devotion propel us forward. This combination is due to grace, and it also brings more grace. At the empirical plane, grace is always essential. Grace to purify the mind. Grace to develop our bond with the *guru*. Grace to follow the *guru*'s instructions, grace to understand the *guru*'s teachings, *grace* to imbibe that understanding. Through and through, grace is needed. As the Upaniṣads say:

> yasya deve parā bhaktiḥ yathā deve tathā gurau | tasyaite kathitā hyārthāḥ prakāśante mahātmanaḥ ||
>
> Only to the great one who has supreme devotion to both God and *guru* is the inner meaning of what is spoken about [in the Upaniṣads] revealed.[4]

As Amma is fond of saying, "It is not enough to say, 'I am *brahman*.' We should express the nature of *brahman* in our actions. Even if someone scolds us, we should be able to remain calm

[4] Śvetāśvatara Upaniṣad, 6.23

without getting angry. We should discriminate, 'I am not the body, I am the *ātmā*. If I am the *ātmā*, then there is no need of sorrow.' A person deserves to be known as one who has attained *brahman* when he has an attitude of non-hatred. In that state, he does not have the feeling of inferior or superior. Everything is within us. We are *brahman*. But it is not enough to merely say so. The feeling of being the *brahman* should arise within us. Both the jackfruit and the seed of the jackfruit are *brahman*. The jackfruit is capable of giving sweetness, but the seed is not. It must sprout, grow, become a tree and then bear jackfruit. Until then, the seed is not the same as the tree or the fruit. The tree is within the seed, but it is in the dormant state. If properly cultivated and looked after, the seed can also become a tree. Likewise, we can also reach the state of *brahman* if we try. What sense is there in calling ourselves *brahman*, we who run after food and clothing while considering the body to be eternal? Look at the *mahātmās*. They have no hatred toward anyone. With a smile, they mingle with everyone. They lead the world looking upon everything with an equal eye. That is what we must follow as an example. First, we need a regular discipline. The fence of regular discipline is needed to protect the young plant of spirituality from the animals of materialism."

Thus, let us strive to understand and assimilate Amma's teachings and those of the scriptures with faith and devotion. Let us ever remain rooted in universal values like compassion, selflessness and humility. Let us develop detachment towards our selfish impulses. Let us serve the world with sincerity, kindness, detachment and care. In this way—with our knowledge firm and our mind becoming ever more and more pure—the divine reality will gradually become a more and more tangible experience for us, within and without. In this way, we will become able to both understand Vedānta and—like Amma—to live Vedānta as well.

In November 2019, Amma was in Europe as part of what would be her final foreign tour before the coronavirus pandemic and the long worldwide lockdowns that followed. At the end of a long *darśan* in Marseille, France, that had been going nonstop since morning, Amma addressed the devotees. Looking at the thousands of people whom she had embraced that day, Amma said, "I see so many of you in sadness. Why are you so sad? If only you could see what I can see. Because I see this infinite, incredible joy that is inside each and every one of you. However, it is coated with layers and layers of sadness; that's why you can't see it. I cannot get it out for you. But for you, it would be so easy. You just have to realize that it's there. It's *there!* It's *there!*"

Amma said that she felt the majority of them understood the essence of Vedānta, but the problem was that their understanding was not rooted in a peaceful and disciplined mind. She then stressed again and again that for the Advaitic self-knowledge to bear fruit, we must first refine and silence the mind through all the various spiritual practices: selfless actions, meditation, values and dispassion, etc.

Even though Amma had given *darśan* continuously for more than 12 hours, and even though the next morning's program was not so far off, Amma then began to sing Nirvāṇa Ṣaṭakam. That is the *stotraṁ* written by Śaṅkarācārya mentioned earlier in this book. The first three quarters of every verse discriminate various aspects of the experienced world—the body, the mind, etc—from the True Self. Then, the final quarter triumphantly proclaims *cid-ānanda-rūpaḥ śivo 'haṁ śivo 'ham*—"I am Śiva, who is of the nature of pure consciousness-bliss, I am Śiva."

Amma told all the devotees that while they sang the *bhajan*, they should close their eyes and allow themselves to forget all of their bonds. Amma said, "The Śiva mentioned here is not Śiva, the God. It refers to the *paramātmā*—the supreme self. At least for the duration of this song, close your eyes and forget that you are 'so and so.' Forget all of that, and as you sing, believe, 'Yes, I am the supreme self. I am the supreme self.'" When Amma sang the *bhajan*, each time the final quarter would return, she would gesture at the devotees and then at her own self as if to say, "It's you! It's me. It's the truth of all of us." *Śivo 'haṁ śivo 'ham.*"

This is the ultimate teaching of Amma and of Advaita: You yourself are the eternal peace and happiness for which you have been searching your entire life. You are not the body or mind. You are pure existence-consciousness-bliss.

You are that one divine thread upon which all hearts are strung. All names and forms arise in you, are sustained in you and merge back into you in an eternal cycle. Pervading everything as its substratum, nothing can ever touch you, much less harm you. You are that truth. "It's you! It's you!"

With Amma's grace, may we all be able to understand, appreciate and live this most sacred truth.

|| oṁ lokāḥ samastāḥ sukhino bhavantu ||
"May all beings everywhere be happy."